WELCOME TO A NE
RUNNING YOUR E

Knowing Your Numbers and mastering them is the key success and enhancing the value of your business.

You will make better decisions based on facts and information rather than guessing – better decisions will result in increased profitability, cash flow, and business/shareholder value. As a result, you will have less stress and owning your own business will be much more enjoyable.

You cannot have financial freedom without financial discipline. I know it works and so do my clients and Know Your Numbers members:

> *"Thank you so much for having me in your group. I have learnt more in two hours than I have in 35 years as a business owner."*

Another business owner of 15 years said *that:*

> *"Know Your Numbers has changed my business and me as a business owner forever."*

You can join them and transform you and your business too. Running a business is not easy – if it was everyone would be doing it.

If you Know Your Numbers and follow the learnings from this book _and apply them_ in your business, your business will change forever, and so will you.

More profit, more cash, a more valuable business and less stress. Who doesn't want that? Read on and I'll show you how.

knowyournumbers.biz

Always remember my 2 Rules for running any business:

Rule 1: Focus on Cash

Rule 2: Don't Forget Rule 1

Know Your Numbers

The three-step playbook for making smarter decisions and making more money

Where Would You Be Now If You Knew This When You Set Up Your Business?

Craig Alexander Rattray

Copyright © 2025 Craig Alexander Rattray Limited

All rights reserved. Without limiting the rights under copyright reserved above, no part of this book may be reproduced, stored, or introduced into a retrieval system, or transmitted, in any form or by any means (electronic, mechanical, photocopying, recording or otherwise), without the prior written permission of both the copyright owner and the publisher.

Published by Craig Alexander Rattray Limited

DISCLAIMER:

This book contains the opinions and ideas of the author. The purpose of this book is to provide you with helpful information. This book should not be relied upon solely to make decisions in your business. Careful attention has been paid to ensure the accuracy of the information, but the author cannot assume responsibility for the validity or consequences of its use. This information is not intended to be all things to all businesses. It is, by nature, generic to most businesses in general.

The material in this book is for informational purposes only. As each individual situation is unique, the author disclaims responsibility for any adverse effects that may result from the use or application of the information contained in this book. Any use of the information found in this book is the sole responsibility of the reader. Any suggestions found in this book are to be followed only after consultation with your own trusted advisors.

DEDICATION AND THANKS

This book is dedicated to my good friend, Gary White, who we lost way too soon. Gary adopted a very similar approach to mine with respect to people and business. He was forward looking and always adding value and helping his clients build value in their businesses. I miss my weekly Zoom meetings with him.

This book is also dedicated to those brave men and women who have made the leap from employment to entrepreneurship. Remember, you are not alone!

If it was easy, everyone would be doing it and there would be no employees.

I would also like to add my thanks to my good friends, Jeff Borschowa and Stephen Arthur. Without their support, guidance, and perseverance, I would never have started this book, never mind complete it. Thank you.

CONTENTS

SECTION 1 - INTRODUCTION 1
    Chapter 1: Why Know Your Numbers? 3
    Chapter 2: The Stages of Business 17
    Chapter 3: Profit and Cash 29
SECTION 2 - WHERE ARE YOU NOW? 45
    Chapter 4: Management Accounts 49
    Chapter 5: Actual versus Budget Variance Analysis 71
    Chapter 6: Key Performance Indicators ("KPIs") 79
SECTION 3 - WHERE HAVE YOU BEEN? 89
    Chapter 7: Prior Years 91
    Chapter 8: Compliance 99
    Chapter 9: Taxation 105
SECTION 4 - WHERE ARE YOU GOING 113
    Chapter 10: Forecasts 115
    Chapter 11: Cash and Funding 127
    Chapter 12: Sale and Exit 143
SECTION 5 – LEARN MORE 157
    Chapter 13: Learn, Apply & Grow 159
    Chapter 14: Know Your Numbers Framework 167
    Chapter 15: What People Say 177
    Chapter 16: You've Read the Book, What Now? 181
SECTION 6 - APPENDICES 187
SECTION 7 – MEET THE AUTHOR 201
SECTION 8 – OTHER BOOKS BY CRAIG ALEXANDER RATTRAY 205

SECTION 1 - INTRODUCTION

"The best time to Know Your Numbers is the day before you set up in business.

The second-best time is now."

Craig Alexander Rattray

NOTES

Chapter 1: Why Know Your Numbers?

Introduction

How many business owners have a financial education?

Very few.

Most set up in business because they are good practically at providing a particular product or service that they have been trained in. They know how to build houses, fix roofs, or have developed a skill in a particular service.

Most people have heard of Warren Buffet. He's worth listening to – he turned $1,000 into hundreds of billions and is one of the richest people on the planet. Despite that, he still lives in the same house he bought in 1958 for $31,500 and goes to McDonald's drive-through for breakfast every morning with the exact money for one of his three daily options ($2.61, $2.95, or $3.17). He will only buy the most expensive option (56 cents higher than the lowest option) if he has had a good trading day the day before and the market is up. This is a man worth billions! He has two rules for investing and I decided that if it worked for him then I should create two rules for my clients and others.

My two rules are:

> Rule 1: Focus on Cash.

> Rule 2: Don't forget Rule 1.

Remember my two rules; they are the keys to your success. More than 20,000 UK companies file for insolvency most years. They generally failed to focus on cash. Don't be like them.

The Reality of Business Ownership

Typically business owners set up in business because they are responding to a change in circumstances or have identified a need for what they do. Examples include falling out with their boss, redundancy, or just the ability to do it for themselves and have freedom.

Unfortunately, freedom is often a long way away.

Why?

Well, mainly because they have no financial education or knowledge of how to run a business, manage cash flow or engage with banks, investors, and accountants.

This creates stress.

Common Challenges

There are many sleepless nights over cash. The business owner is last to be paid (if at all) and they are generally working more hours than when they were employed.

Lots of stress and sleepless nights.

Running on empty – both in terms of energy and the bank account.

Is that you?

Does it sound familiar?

If so, please read on.

Purpose of This Book

This is not another book on accounting or finance. It is a book specifically aimed at you – the business owner.

It is a practical guide to making your business better and making owning a business more enjoyable.

I believe that it is a must-read for all business owners.

My Promise

This book will show that it is possible, and actually reasonably simple, to Know Your Numbers and make better decisions based on the right financial information.

You will understand the financial information and understand what areas to monitor, manage and how to use it to run your business.

You will make better decisions as a result of having this information and understanding it.

The book will show you how to:

- Prevent financial mistakes.
- Resolve financial mistakes.
- Resolve the many financial headaches you have in your business because you have not been trained in finance.

If you follow this book, you will not only reduce stress, but you'll make more profit, generate more cash flow, and build a more valuable business.

Steps to Success

You can do all of this if you:

- Learn – by reading the book.
- Apply – taking the learnings and putting them in place in your business, and,
- Grow – both you and your business.

It really is that simple.

About Know Your Numbers

I created Know Your Numbers for business owners like you – those with little or no financial education and poorly served by accountants, finance directors and finance people in general.

Most of these finance professionals like to pretend that finance is difficult and that there is a mystique and a black art to it.

Nonsense!

This may be controversial, but I believe that a large part of accountancy has been created by the accountancy profession to create a profession.

A profession that only serves accountants, not business owners.

My Approach
I make accounting and finance simple. It is simple. Please trust me.

Someone once told me during a podcast interview that I take a very complex subject and make it very simple.

I disagreed. I said that it is a simple subject that is unnecessarily complicated by accountants and finance professionals.

So please keep that in mind as you work your way through this book.

When you apply these learnings, the impact can be profound. I received an email from a member after his first Know Your Numbers Mastery session saying "Thank you so much for having me in your group. I have learnt more in two hours than I have in 35 years as a business owner."

Another business owner of 15 years said that "Know Your Numbers has changed my business and me as a business owner forever".

If you want to hear stories from some of the people who have been on our KYN Mastery Groups, you can find them here at knowyournumbers.biz/stories.

Overcoming Fear of Numbers

The fear of numbers and finance often goes back to school days when the maths teacher made you feel stupid because you couldn't quickly grasp the subject.

But was it you, or was it a poor teacher?

Our Know Your Numbers groups operate on the basis that there are no stupid questions. I have not been trained in building houses or fixing roofs so my operational questions are on the basis of little or no knowledge.

The same applies to your questions on finance. You have not been trained in it – there are no stupid questions.

Give yourself the freedom to open your mind to understanding and Knowing Your Numbers. As I have shown many times, it is not difficult.

Know Your Numbers is the framework to your success.

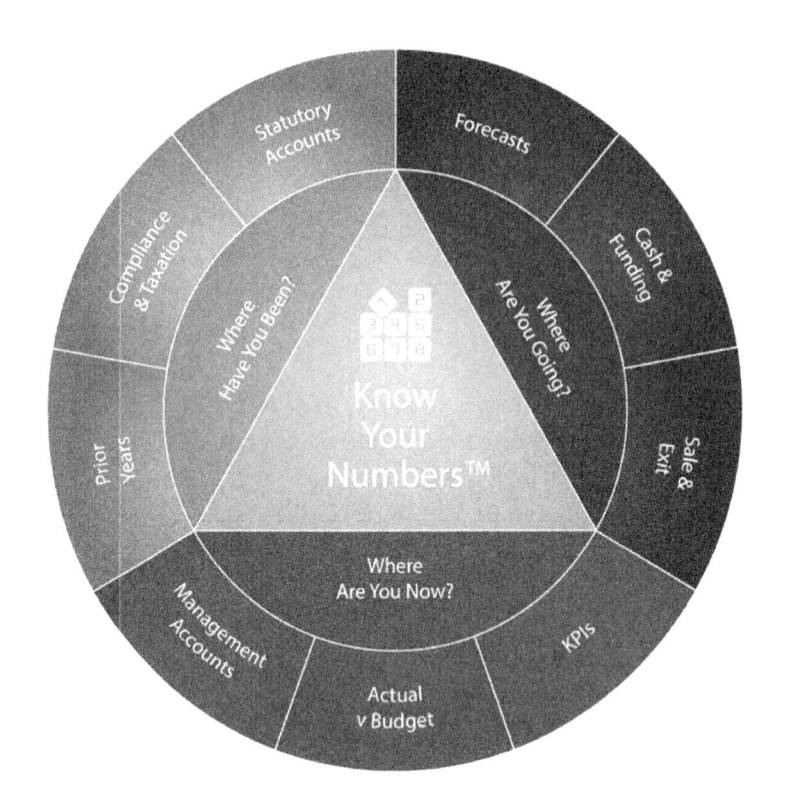

The Power of Financial Understanding

If you learn this, you will understand the financial information you need to understand:

- Where are you now?
- Where have you been?
- Where are you going?

Learn this, apply it and you and your business will grow.

- Learn
- Apply, and
- Grow

Adopting the Framework
If you adopt this framework in your business, you will have better information which will lead to better decisions.

It will remove pain and constraints.

Too many business owners are completely stressed.

Business should be fun and profitable at the same time.

Reflecting on Past Decisions
Think about how your business would be different if you had better information on which to base previous decisions you have made.

- Would you have made the same decision?
- How would things be different?
- Would you have made more money, or perhaps lost less money?

If you get this right, it will lead to increased profitability, cash flow and make your business more valuable.

That's most definitely a winning combination, with the added bonus of significantly less stress.

Mindset and Growth Opportunities
Many business owners have a fixed mindset. I assume that you don't because you are reading this book.

Many business owners don't understand how to take advantage of growth opportunities and how to finance their business.

Webinar Invitation
I've created a free online 20-minute webinar (available at kynmastery.com/kyn-book-resources) called "Better Decisions, More Money."

It focuses on making smarter, informed decisions using the Know Your Numbers Framework to unlock growth and increase profitability. By improving your cash flow and decision-making, you'll reduce stress, work smarter, and take more home at the end of the day.

It makes running your business simpler and more rewarding.

Is that something you'd find valuable? Then go to the resources page and check it out!

The Two Weakest Areas

The two weakest areas in most businesses are:

1. Finance
2. Your own psychology

They also cause the most pain.

When I refer to finance, I mean both the understanding of finance and the quality of the financial information as well as the funding that is in place.

You must get your mindset right or nothing else matters.

Think positively, think creatively, adopt an abundance mindset, and solve problems for your clients and customers.

Reflect on Decisions

Close your eyes for a few seconds and think about this.

Can you think of a decision you have made in your business that you would change if you were to go back and have the right information available to you?

How much would that be worth to you?

The Know Your Numbers Framework is all about providing you with better information to make better decisions.

The Finance Function

In most businesses the finance function is the weakest areas of the business.

Why?

Quite simply, most business owners have established their business because they are good at the operational side of the business. However, they have never been trained in finance.

Can I ask you another question? Why did you set up your business?

The answers will vary and will include:

- Identifying an opportunity.
- Frustration with your current employer/boss.
- To increase wealth and pay yourself more.

The last one doesn't usually happen for a while, if ever in many cases.

What typically happens when most people start their own business is that they end up paying themselves less due to a lack of cash.

Typically, they are last to be paid and usually paid less than when they were employed.

I want to change that and want to help you understand why it happens.

Trademarked Methodology

Follow my trademarked methodology and understand the information you need to run your business and make better decisions:

I want to change that and want to help you to have a well-functioning finance function that provides you with the information you need to run your business and to make better decisions, and to increase your wealth and pay yourself more.

Better decisions will lead to improved profitability, cash flow, and shareholder value.

Engagement and Understanding

As you read this book, please take notes, and also think about these two questions:

1. How does this apply to me?
2. Do I understand this?

If you don't understand it, please reread it and if you still don't, please contact me and I will assist.

Approach to Learning

I want you to adopt a "Learn, Apply and Grow" approach:

- Learn from reading the book.
- Apply it in your business.
- Grow as a result of having better information and being able to fund your business for growth.

Action is Essential

Understanding this is a means to an end. It is great that you will be able to understand, but it's reasonably worthless if you don't apply it in your business and improve your understanding of how it applies to your business.

You must do the work and take action. Otherwise, you will still be where you are now.

Is that what you want?

This is not difficult. I promise.

Come with me and I'll show you how to change your business and your life for the better.

Embrace the Journey

Let's go! Knowing Your Numbers is not just about being better informed—it's about being better equipped to lead your business toward a prosperous future. Reflect on your understanding and prepare to dive deeper into the world of financial mastery in the coming chapters.

Before you turn the page, take a moment. Consider your current financial know-how. Are you in control, or are you avoiding the numbers?

Let's change that. By the end of this book, you will not only understand your numbers; you will be eager to use them.

Frequently Asked Questions

The following FAQs are designed to reinforce key concepts covered in this chapter. While some information may seem repetitive, it is intentionally included to enhance learning and retention.

Question: What are the most common misconceptions or mistakes businesses make related to this topic that you want to highlight?

Answer: One of the most common misconceptions is that Knowing Your Numbers is only important for large businesses. Businesses of all sizes need to understand their financials to thrive. Many small business owners fail to track their expenses and revenue accurately and far fewer have forecasts in place, leading to cash flow problems and missed growth opportunities. By emphasising the importance of financial literacy and forward-looking forecasting, we aim to help businesses avoid these pitfalls. Another is that they have an accountant or bookkeeper, so they don't need to know and understand their numbers. It is your business and your numbers. It is your responsibility. Know Your Numbers, Know Your Business.

Question: How have businesses transformed after understanding and applying this principle?

Answer: I think applying the principles in the book is a no-brainer for any business. Any businesses that have embraced and applied them have seen significant transformations. For instance, many have achieved substantial growth by closely monitoring their financial metrics. By understanding their cash flow, profit margins, and other key indicators, these businesses were able to secure necessary funding, optimise their operations, and ultimately increase their profitability. Most business owners who embrace Know Your Numbers are happier, make more money, and have less stress.

Listen to how it's impacted the lives of the business owners who have applied these principles on our website knowyournumbers.biz/stories.

Question: What specific financial practices should businesses adopt to start "Knowing Their Numbers"?

Answer: Do everything every day. To start "Knowing Their Numbers," businesses should adopt several key financial practices. These include maintaining up-to-date accounting records, regularly reviewing financial statements, and implementing a cash flow forecast. Daily financial management practices, such as tracking expenses and revenues, reconciling bank statements, processing purchase invoices, issuing sales invoices and monitoring key performance indicators, are essential for staying on top of your business's financial health. Also, answer my 3 daily questions every day.

Download The 3 Questions PDF here: kynmastery.com/kyn-book-resources

Action Items
- Remember my 2 Rules for any business.
- Learn the Know your Numbers framework and apply it in your business.
- Download the 3 Daily Questions PDF and ask the three questions in your business daily.

NOTES

Chapter 2: The Stages of Business

NOTES

I assume if you are reading this then you are a business owner. However, are you really a business owner or do you have a job?

Two simple definitions to think about as you read through this book:

- **Job** – a paid position of regular employment or work done for pay.
- **Business** – a commercial activity.

Whilst different people have different definitions for the stages of business, I want to emphasise the 3 stages that I like to focus on.

The key is changing from being an Operator (and working in the business) to becoming an Entrepreneur (and working on the business).

Stage 1: Birth to Toddler

This is the start-up phase and early development of the business.

- Typically, start-up to turnover of around £1.5m.
- The focus here is on transactions and turnover.
- There is an income generation focus rather than profitability and cash.
- Typically, you do everything yourself because you have limited cash.
- There is no communication strategy.
- You are working in the business and not on the business.
- It's the "kitchen table" approach.

- There is no or limited infrastructure, again because of a lack of cash.
- No systems.
- No board or good advisors.
- No Finance Director or Chief Financial Officer – these roles are seen as a cost rather than an investment.
- You don't know what you don't know.
- There is no funding in the business. It's all from earnings or personal savings.
- Unstructured.
- Unplanned.
- No or limited financial information.
- No budgets.
- No forecasts.
- Very little is measured – remember, you can't manage what you don't measure.
- You live day to day.
- Lots of uncertainty, chaos, and pain – you feel as if you are working every hour.
- You spend most days putting out fires and living from day to day.
- The business runs you.

This stage of development has lots of pain and a scarcity mindset prevails.

Stage 2: Teenager to Young Adult

This is the next phase as the business grows and develops.

- It is typically from £1m to £3m of turnover.
- Pain has resulted in some changes.
- However, there remains a lot of constraints and a lack of visibility.
- You are still working in the business – you're trying to work on it, but are too busy operationally.
- A lack of cash and funding is preventing the addition of new employees, so your solution is to work more and pay yourself less.
- Improvements are required.
- However, you still don't know what you don't know.
- There is demand for the business and your services, but you are unable to provide the services due to constraints – again as a result of a lack of cash.
- The ability to fund support is limited and probably getting worse.
- There is an increasing demand for cash and despite working all hours and "making money" you feel worse off.
- There is no strong relationship with your accountant other than transactional and usually a year end with tax and compliance focus.
- It is reactive at best.

- Your accountant doesn't properly know or understand either you or your business, or your people, and has no idea about growth and funding.
- You are doing even more.
- Stress is increasing.
- You are tired and struggling to cope.
- Cash is even more constrained as a result of the growth.
- Thers is still no Finance Director and no forecasting.
- You're still running blind and no clear idea where you are going financially.
- You still think of a Finance Director as a cost rather than as an investment.
- You are not thinking exit or life plan or wealth plan.
- You're thinking survival and how to get through another week or month.
- When will it end?
- There is a massive impact on you and your personal life.

This stage of development has you still working in the business with a lack of cash even more of an issue. The challenge is to move from there to have more cash/funding and to build a team. You need a properly funded business.

Stage 3: Adulthood to Maturity

This is where you want to be, and it doesn't necessarily need to be at a higher level of turnover.

- It is a mindset and a way of running your business.

- I have clients and Know Your Numbers members who have reached this by changing their mindset and taking the right action, at levels of turnover I mention at stages one and two.
- It is not the turnover that is the key factor.
- It is you.
- There is a change.
- You make the move from a lifestyle business to what I call a proper business.
- You put the right infrastructure in place.
- You introduce financial systems and procedures.
- You think about funding.
- You introduce a part-time Finance Director to oversee this and assist you.
- Hiring a part-time Finance Director becomes "a no brainer" as it is required to make your life easier, your business worth more money and to reduce your stress.
- It is required to guide the Financial Strategy.
- You start to work on the business.
- The funding allows you to hire the right operational and strategic team.
- You are leading.
- You are thinking about your Growth and Exit strategy.
- You have effective Financial Management and the right Funding in place.

- You have removed pain and blockages.
- There is always a conflict between growth and control – more growth usually means less control.
- That makes Knowing Your Numbers even more important because growth creates more of a working capital requirement.
- Working capital is the cash or finance facilities that are essential for running the day-to-day operations of a business and meeting its obligations.

As the business grows it typically needs an ever-increasing amount of working capital. We will discuss that in more detail later.

Change!

I want to change you from an Operator to an Entrepreneur. This is what the third stage is all about.

Stop doing - start thinking and leading.

This is the place you want to be.

- Less stress.
- More money.
- A more valuable business.

It is all possible if you Learn, Apply and Grow as this book shows you.

Opportunity without structure is chaos – you must instil discipline and structure in your business.

That is the price of freedom and growth.

If you Know your Numbers and have the right financial information you remove much of the risk and uncertainty.

You move into a position of control and more confidence.

Knowing Your Numbers gives you Clarity, Certainty and Visibility.

Conclusion

In wrapping up, we will review the journey through each stage of business. We will emphasise that Knowing Your Numbers isn't just for accountants—it's for every business owner intent on success.

Consider where you stand in the lifecycle of your business. Is it time for a change? Is your financial understanding sufficient for the challenges ahead? Use our self-assessment tool to gain clarity on your business's current phase. You can find our self-assessment tool here: kynmastery.com/kyn-book-resources.

Frequently Asked Questions

Question: Can you provide detailed descriptions or characteristics of each business stage?

Answer: Each business stage has distinct characteristics and challenges. In this chapter, we describe our way of thinking about the typical stages of business growth, from startup to maturity. For example, during the startup stage, businesses often focus on establishing a market presence and developing a customer base. As they grow, they need to focus on scaling operations and managing increased complexity. By understanding these stages, business owners can better prepare for the transitions and challenges they will face.

Question: How should businesses adapt their strategies at different stages?

Answer: While the core principle of Knowing Your Numbers remains the same, the strategies businesses use should evolve as they grow. For instance, a startup might focus on cash flow management and customer acquisition, while a growing business might prioritise optimising operations, profitability, and securing funding for expansion. By regularly reviewing their financial data and adjusting their strategies accordingly, businesses can navigate each stage more effectively.

Question: What are the key indicators that a business is transitioning between stages?

Answer: Key indicators of a business transitioning between stages include changes in revenue, cash flow, and operational complexity including the need for more people and capital expenditure or investment. For example, an increase in working capital requirements often signals that a business is growing and needs additional resources to support that growth. By monitoring these indicators, business owners can anticipate the need for additional funding and make proactive decisions to support their continued growth.

Question: Can you discuss any personal experiences or case studies related to navigating these stages?

Answer: Most business owners that approach me or join Know Your Numbers have profit/growth, people and/or stress challenges – most of which can be resolved by cash and the right funding. By implementing effective financial management practices and securing necessary funding, they were able to overcome these challenges and continue their growth trajectory. These real-world examples provide valuable insights into the practical application of the principles discussed in this book. I also share stories from the entrepreneurs that I have worked with in our Know Your Numbers Groups. You can check out their stories here:

kynmastery.com/kyn-book-resources.

Action Items
- Understand what stage your business is at.
- Move from being an Operator and become an Entrepreneur.
- Make better decisions based on better information.

NOTES

Chapter 3: Profit and Cash

I'll start this chapter repeating my 2 Rules for running any business.

Rule 1: Focus on Cash

Rule 2: Don't forget Rule 1

I give credit to Warren Buffet for inspiring this as it is based on his 2 rules for investing. For me, the 2 rules emphasise the importance of cash in any business.

NOTES

Importance of Cash

My first two books were based on cash flow and were both Number 1 Hot New Releases on Amazon.

Mastering Cash Flow for Business Owners is available on Amazon and can also be downloaded for free at masteringcashflowbook.com.

I encourage you to read *Mastering Cash Flow for Business Owners* in conjunction with this book. It will make a huge difference to you and your business.

Rather than recreating a lot of this, I am going to include some of the key parts below.

Please remember always – **profit is not the same as cash**.

Profit does not pay the wages or the suppliers.

Cash does.

What is Cash Flow?

Simply, cash flow is the flow of cash into and out of your business.

Think of cash flow in a similar way to fuel in your car or oxygen in the atmosphere – run out of fuel and the car stops, run out of oxygen and we die.

Run out of cash and your business dies.

I love this quote from Michael Dell, founder and CEO, Dell Technologies who perfectly sums up the approach of many business owners:

"We were always focused on our profit and loss statement. But cash flow was not a regularly discussed topic. It was as if we were driving along, watching only the speedometer, when in fact we were running out of gas."

I hope that you understand this and how it emphasises the difference between profit and cash.

The Challenge of Positive Cash Flow

All businesses should aim for positive cash flow by generating more cash (inflows) than they are spending (outflows), but that is not always possible as the business grows. As the business grows the working capital requirement increases.

What does this mean?

In simplistic terms, you need more cash or finance facilities in your business as you are funding higher levels of revenue and the related costs.

Understanding Working Capital

Think about your own business.

Do you offer credit terms?

Yes?

If so, do you usually need to pay your employees and suppliers before you are paid in full?

That cash requirement is the **working capital**, and as you grow on that basis, it increases.

It makes running a growing business more challenging.

However, if cash is monitored and forecast, it can be managed – if you don't monitor it then you can't manage it.

The best way to generate cash is to have a profitable business, and to understand the many and varied cash flows and their timings.

The Importance of Cash Flow Management

The *Mastering Cash Flow* book cites various statistics about the importance of cash and what happens if you don't follow my 2 Rules.

Some of the statistics are frightening.

As a business owner you need to avoid becoming another of these statistics.

Real-World Statistics

The Intuit whitepaper, "QuickBooks State of Cash Flow Report," states that 62% of all businesses admit to experiencing a cash flow shortfall, or nearly running out of money.

A Fin Pacific study stated that "69% of business owners report having sleepless nights over their cash flow".

I do not know of any business owner who has never had cash flow issues that keep them awake at night.

Are you another?

A US Bank study stated that 83% of business failures cited poor cash management as a key factor (Dryrun.com).

In "QuickBooks State of Cash Flow Report," of the 44% of businesses that ran out of money, nearly half were taken completely by surprise.

By surprise – really?

That is a real concern.

The Need for Better Cash Management

Nearly 30% of all businesses will die due to cash flow issues, yet according to a study by Intuit, 83% of businesses owners possessed a basic or failing grade of financial literacy.

Know Your Numbers

Even more worryingly, a business owner does not need to have to run out of cash to feel stress. The Intuit report goes beyond the chance of shortfalls and probes into the stress it puts on business owners. A staggering 80% report feeling stress over their cash flow whether they have run short or not.

Example: "Bill & Melinda"

Whilst my focus with clients is usually Strategic Finance, my role can also be that of a social worker, doctor, and even a marriage guidance counsellor. Let me tell you about a husband and wife – let's call them Bill & Melinda. They were always on the cash rollercoaster and always in conflict and stress as a result.

I first met Bill, and he told me of the opportunities. I asked him what his aim was in 5 years – £5M.

I laughed and asked, "why not £5M in 2 years based on what you've just told me?"

Bill laughed.

I said, "I don't know your business, but it's people and cash."

He nodded.

I said, "if what you've told me is right, I'll get you there in 2 years."

He stood up, shook my hand, and said, "You're in."

We achieved £5.5 million within 5 years and an EBITDA of 10X plus.

Addressing Cash Flow Issues

How do you address these issues and avoid being another statistic?

You must manage your cash flow.

What does that mean and how do you do it?

What is Cash Flow Management?

Quite simply cash flow management is a set of procedures, policies and actions that allow a business owner to track, understand, and improve cash flow.

The goal of cash flow management is to be able to control cash and to forecast cash inflows and outflows accurately.

Any business owner must understand the cash inflows, the cash outflows, and the precise cash position on an ongoing basis. That is the key to effective cash flow management.

Benefits of Cash Flow Management

By preparing in advance with cash flow management, shortfalls can be highlighted, action taken, and the business can continue to trade on a satisfactory basis whilst keeping all suppliers and employees happy and paid on time.

Successful cash flow management predicts cash inflows, cash outflows and the future cash position whether that is an excess or a shortfall.

According to a study by Fin Pacific, businesses managing their cash flow monthly have an 80% survival rate versus businesses that rely on cash flow planning as an annual activity. That percentage increases by managing cash flow daily or even weekly.

80% is huge.

You want to be one of the 80 and not the 20.

Why is Cash Important?
Many business owners fail to understand that there is a difference between profit and cash.

If you own a profitable business and were paid for all sales immediately you would never have a cash flow problem.

However, as we all know most businesses make sales and provide credit terms so whilst the sale is made today, the cash may not be received for 30 days or more.

No business can survive without cash (or adequate bank facilities).

If your company is making losses, then it will inevitably consume cash, so the starting point is to ensure that you have a profitable business, although that falls outside the scope of this book. Although by Knowing Your Numbers you will be on top of that and will be able to do something about it.

For this book's purposes we will assume that you own a profitable business.

What does it mean to own a profitable business?
Profit is the difference between the total of all sales less the total of all costs and expenses for a particular period.

Many business owners may realise at some stage that that the profit they make in the business does not equal their cash flow, unless they are dealing solely in cash which is unlikely today.

However, even profitable businesses cannot survive without cash – as we said earlier, think of cash as the oxygen a business needs to stay alive.

Funding Costs

A sale can be made today generating the profit, but the cash may not be received for perhaps 30 days or more.

How do you fund the costs during that intervening period? You probably have employees to pay; rent on premises; materials and other costs used to generate the sale; and other business overheads.

There will also be sales tax and corporate taxes which will fall due later – please never forget these and make sure they are forecast and managed.

It is vital to understand timings of cash flow both in and out.

If that is all true and important, then why does everyone not forecast cash flow?

That is the key question.

In my view it is madness not to.

Running a Business Without Cash Forecast

Another question. How do you run a business without a cash forecast?

Answer. Badly.

I fail to understand how you can run a business without forecasting cash, other than badly.

However, most businesses do not actively manage their cash flow.

If in doubt, remember the phrase "cash is king" – like most popular phrases it has been created for a reason and it is true.

A similar saying is that "revenue is vanity, profit is sanity and cash flow is reality." Also true.

Very few successful businesses do not actively manage their cash flow, and similarly very few failing businesses actively manage their cash flow. Trust me, there is a pattern here!

The Role of Cash Flow Management

There are many business owners who do not want to know or tell me that they do not have the time to actively manage their cash flow.

I am sorry, but that is complete nonsense.

If there is only one thing you do financially, make it managing cash flow.

This again comes back to the business owner does not know what they do not know.

This book seeks to change that.

I believe that the biggest reason for not managing cash flow is that you, the business owner, do not know where to start and do not properly understand cash flow.

Managing cash flow can also help you and your management team identify problems in the business faster than any other diagnostic tool.

Understanding the Difference Between Cash and Profit

Here is another frightening statistic: A study from Fin Pacific stated that 70% of businesses that fail were profitable when they ceased trading. Profitable and they failed? Really? Yes.

If you needed more evidence on the difference between cash and profit, surely that is it.

Again – 70% of businesses in the study were profitable when they failed – wow!

So why did they fail? Cash Flow.

These businesses failed to match their cash outflows with cash inflows and did not have an adequate cash buffer or working capital facility.

Simple.

How could that be avoided?

Simple.

Better cash management; use of real-time historic financial information; and good forecasts. For good forecasts, in particular a weekly rolling cash flow model shows the peaks and troughs over the forthcoming period.

If you do not measure cash flow, you will not be able to manage it effectively and make the right decisions.

Without that tool, you may well spend money next week that you need the following week.

How will you know without a weekly forecast?

Cash flow management and planning reduces stress and improves your chances of success. It puts the business owner in control of an area that many business owners neglect.

Remember, cash flow worries are the biggest area that keeps business owners awake at night. Effective cash management will change that and make the future even brighter than the past. This means lots of restful nights with no cash worries.

Key Principles of Cash Flow Management
There are 3 things to remember:

1. If you do not make a profit you will not generate positive cash flow from trading.

2. Without up-to-date historic figures, your current cash position, and a forecast, you will never be able to manage cash flow optimally and effectively.

3. Cash is King.

Daily Cash Flow Management

Ask yourself my three Daily Questions – this is a must for your business.

I like my clients to ask themselves these 3 questions every morning at the start of each day.

This creates a focus on cash and is a constant reminder of the importance of cash.

Question1: How much cash do we have?

Simple, log onto your online banking or online accounting if you have an automatic feed and you will see the position.

Reconcile the bank account(s) and your aged trade debtors (money owed to you by your customers) and your aged trade creditors (money you owe to suppliers) will be up-to-date.

Question 2: Who has our cash?

This is found in the trade debtors report that you have updated as part of question 1.

Review it. Who has not paid yet? Who is late? Ask them for it. Chase it.

Have a clearly defined credit control policy from the start of the process (taking on a new client) to the end point where they pay you.

Make sure everyone knows their role and plays their part. The *Mastering Cash Flow* book has a section devoted to "Cash Inflows" and provides a lot of tips and insight.

Question 3: How do we get more cash?

I like to have a series of Key Performance Indicators (KPIs) that track this and focus on profit and cash generation.

My favourite KPIs for this include gross margin, trade debtor days, and EBITDA.

Remember this. Cash in is either income or is creating a liability. Cash out is reducing a liability by paying costs or debt, or creating an asset.

In my view, a sale is not a sale until you have collected the cash.

Remember my two rules for running any business:

Rule 1: Focus on Cash

Rule 2: Don't forget Rule 1

Cash and Funding is discussed further in Chapter 11.

These three questions are available as a download at kynmastery.com/kyn-book-resources.

Conclusion

The message is clear: Profit is a measure of success, but cash flow is the enabler of it. Mastering both is not optional; it's essential. As you close this chapter, consider your own business' financial pulse and what steps you can take to strengthen it.

Take a moment now to look at your financial statements. Can you identify your profit margins? Do you know your cash flow cycles? Use the tools provided to start taking control of these critical numbers today.

Frequently Asked Questions

Question: What key points should be emphasised when discussing the relationship between profit and cash flow?

Answer: It is crucial to understand that profit and cash flow are not the same. A business can be profitable on paper but still face cash flow issues if it doesn't manage its working capital effectively or plan for growth with increased working capital facilities. Key points to emphasise include the importance of timely collection of receivables, efficient management of payables, and maintaining optimal inventory levels. These practices help ensure that a business has enough cash on hand to meet its obligations and invest in growth opportunities.

Question: Are there particular strategies or tools you recommend for managing these effectively?

Answer: Effective cash flow management requires a combination of strategies and tools. One approach is to use my three daily questions:

- How much cash do we have?
- Who's got our cash?
- How can we improve our cash position?

Additionally, adhering to the two rules of focusing on cash and not forgetting rule one helps maintain a strong cash flow position. Tools like cash flow forecasts, budgeting software, and regular financial reviews are also essential. These are discussed later.

Question: What are some common pitfalls in cash flow management that businesses should avoid?

Answer: Common pitfalls in cash flow management include failing to forecast cash flow, neglecting to actively manage cash flow, and not having adequate working capital facilities. These issues can lead to cash shortages, missed opportunities, and financial instability as well as stress and sleepless nights. By proactively forecasting and managing cash flow, businesses can avoid these pitfalls and maintain a healthy financial position.

Question: Could you provide insights into balancing profit generation with maintaining adequate cash reserves?

Answer: Balancing profit generation with maintaining adequate cash reserves requires careful planning and foresight. The Know Your Numbers framework helps businesses understand their current and future financial needs, allowing them to arrange adequate working capital facilities in advance. By forecasting cash flow and regularly reviewing financial performance, businesses can ensure they have enough cash and working capital facilities on hand to support ongoing operations and invest in growth opportunities.

Action Items

- Understand the difference between profit and cash.
- Understand your cash in flows and out flows.
- Read Mastering Cash Flow for Business Owners.

NOTES

SECTION 2 - WHERE ARE YOU NOW?

NOTES

Do you understand where you are today from a financial perspective?

You are the business owner – it is your responsibility. If you don't know, why not?

I am a great believer in doing everything every day.

I learned that in 1994 from one of my first bosses: "If you do everything every day, then you are only a day behind". Very true.

It makes complete sense.

It was more challenging to do this 30 years ago because we did not have online banking and online accounting.

However, it was still possible and it was the approach I adopted then, and still do to this day.

There are no longer any excuses as we have online accounting and online banking. Real time up-to-date information is not something you should aspire to. It is something you must have. It is essential for success.

Like all of these things, it is not difficult if you adopt the "do everything every day" approach.

- Reconcile the bank. Remember my 3 daily questions?
- Issue customer invoices.
- Process supplier invoices.

Where is the difficulty in that?

Like all journeys, the map is useless if we have the wrong starting position.

Where you are now ensures that we know where we are today and gives us the correct starting point for our journey and our forecast.

I spend very little time looking back, as for me, the key to success is looking forward – that is why Section 4 "Where Are You Going?" is my favourite and it is where I like to spend most of my time with clients and Know Your Numbers members.

However, without knowing "where are we now" then the "where are we going" part becomes difficult.

A good Finance Director and/or Finance Team provides information to allow you to run the business better.

In my view, the key purpose of the Finance Team is to provide information to the operational team and the strategic team to allow them to run the business and make better decisions.

I encourage you to embrace the "do everything every day" approach and see what a difference it makes in your business.

"Where are you now" refers to management accounts, actual against budget variance analysis and Key Performance Indicators.

This section discusses it in detail and shows what you must do and what you must have in place.

Chapter 4: Management Accounts

NOTES

Have you ever seen the dashboard of a plane? There are lots of dials and information. It looks confusing.

The pilot uses it to guide the plane and to reach the chosen destination.

Without the dashboard, the pilot would be running blind and the chances of getting to your destination would be very slim.

The dashboard is not confusing to the pilot as he understands it and knows where everything is.

He knows when to react to changes and to different information.

He uses the information from the dashboard to make better decisions and to reach the destination.

It could be said that the chances of surviving the flight without the dashboard would be remote, too.

Think of your business. Do you have a dashboard?

You may have some financial information, but is it confusing to you?

Do you have the right information to take you on your journey or is your business not going to make it?

The dashboard for your business is management accounts and related information.

What are Management Accounts?
Quite simply, management accounts are accounts and other financial information that are prepared to show the trading performance of a business. They are your dashboard. They show you where you are and provide the latest information for the business.

Know Your Numbers

Yes, but what are accounts?
We'll answer that very soon below.

For the typical business owner accounts are something new. As I stated before, most business owners have never been educated in accounting and finance.

Typically, the business owner is skilled in the operational side of the business, not in running and managing a business and understanding the financial aspects of it.

As I have said, this is not another book on accounting. However, it is important that I explain, and you understand, what accounts are.

I will explain that below, but first, why should we prepare management accounts and what are they? Management accounts are prepared to understand how the business has traded and its financial position. It is the company's dashboard and shows where you are. Management accounts are used to evaluate performance, drive performance and to create accountability. They should be up-to-date and as real time as possible.

Why Real Time?
If the information is late then you lose the opportunity to use it to make better decisions and to change things.

Think of two situations. One where you have management accounts within a week of the end of the month and the other where you have management accounts four weeks after the end of the month. In the first scenario, you still have three weeks or more to make changes and influence the performance of the current month. In the second scenario you have lost that opportunity to change and influence performance.

Up-to-date management accounts let you know where you are now and give you that clarity and certainty, as well as the visibility of the current position.

I like to ask business owners, "how do you know if you have a good day/week/month?"

The responses are usually based on comments like, all of my employees are on site, all of my vehicles are on hire, or the phones are constantly ringing.

Yes, I hear that and understand that, but it doesn't tell me financially how well you have performed – that is where management accounts are important (and Key Performance Indicators or KPIs too as we will cover in chapter 6).

Show how well you are performing based on information and metrics not instinct and "gut feel."

Use the financial information and ensure you have the right things in place to monitor, manage and improve.

We want to understand the current position and how we can make changes going forward that will improve performance and increase profitability, cash flow, and business/shareholder value.

Management Accounts allow us to make Better Decisions.

How? They show how you have performed for a certain period and your financial position at a point in time.

Knowing Your Numbers and knowing each part of your business is critical to success.

Whilst it is good to know the overall performance of your business, it is even better if you know how each constituent part has performed – product, service line, project, or indeed customer/client, or employee.

This provides even better information and allows you to make changes.

Without getting too technical, the Pareto Principle (also known as the "80/20 rule") states that for many outcomes, roughly 80% of consequences come from 20% of causes.

What does this mean for your business?
It means that 20% of your products or services are likely to contribute 80% of your profit; 20% of your sales team are likely to deliver 80% of the sales, and probably more importantly, that 80% of your products/services will only contribute 20% of your profit.

What should you do with that information?
Well, my approach with my clients is to regularly (normally quarterly, but at least annually) review the products/services/customer base and get rid of the bottom 20%.

By having the detailed analysis of this information, you can make better decisions and decide to stop working with certain customers, increase prices or indeed, just continue as is.

However, at least you will be doing it from a position of information and will have based that decision on it. Rather than operating in blissful ignorance.

It's your business, it is up to you.

It has been said that doing ordinary things consistently produces extraordinary results. Doing everything every day is ordinary. Keep doing these ordinary things daily and you will produce extraordinary results.

So, to the question I asked above, what are accounts?

Accounts typically comprise a profit and loss account (or income statement or trading account) and a balance sheet (or statement of financial position).

I like to think of the profit and loss as a video of what has happened over the period/month/year and the balance sheet as a still photograph at a point in time.

Whilst you do not need to know all of the details, it is important to understand what each statement does and the format of it.

Then you can establish how to monitor, manage, and influence some of the key components within each statement.

Profit and Loss Account or Income Statement
A profit and loss account or income statement covers the trading for a period of time and shows all sales or income less all costs thereby establishing whether a profit or loss has been made.

All figures are shown net of Value Added Tax – remember VAT is not your money and you are only collecting it on behalf of the government/HM Revenue and Customs. I encourage my clients to set up a separate bank account (the number 2 account) to retain the cash there. I am not saying you can't use it for working capital purposes, but be mindful, always, that it is not your money.

It could be argued that it should be called a profit "or" loss account rather than a profit "and" loss account as the business cannot make a profit and a loss, but let's not dwell on that!

Think of this statement as a video with a start point and an end point covering a period of time. Typically, this is prepared monthly and annually, but it could be weekly or even daily.

The structure can vary, but is typically set out like this and I like to think of it in 3 parts.

- Sales to Gross Profit
- Overheads or infrastructure costs to reach EBITDA
- ITDA costs to retained profit and include dividends

These sections are explained in more detail below.

Part 1: Sales to Gross Profit

Sales or income/revenue – this includes all sales that have been invoiced in the period whether they have been paid or not. It can also include an adjustment for work done, but not yet invoiced (known as work in progress or accrued income). Basically, it includes the revenue transactions connected with the commercial activity of the business.

One key point to make here is that if you do not calculate work-in-progress or accrued income every month then your sales figure (and gross profit) will be wrong, and your accounts are probably misleading. If you have done work for a client and not invoiced it then it is work-in-progress or accrued income – you will have included the costs (in cost of sales below), but will not have matched it correctly with the revenue. I explain this in Section 6 Appendices.

Cost of sales or direct costs - These are the costs that the business has incurred to make the sales and only happen as a direct result of the sale. Think of a house building business. The direct costs are the costs of building the house – the labour, materials, subcontractors, and other directly attributable costs of constructing the house.

Gross profit – this is the difference between the sales and the direct costs.

Gross Margin – this is the gross profit expressed as a percentage of sales. The higher this is then the more differentiated your business is and the more your business is a price setter rather than a price taker. This is discussed in more detail at Chapter 12 Sale and Exit. This "pricing power" is attractive to acquirers and increases the strategic value of the business as well as having a hugely positive impact on profitability and cash flow.

Please remember not to confuse Gross Margin with Mark Up.

Gross Margin is based on sales price and Mark-Up is based on cost price. As a result, the Gross Margin percentage will always be lower than the Mark Up percentage.

Learn this and make sure you are not speaking at crossed purposes when discussing it.

Appendix 5 shows a table summarising the difference between Gross Margin and Mark Up.

Part 2: Overheads

This covers the overheads of the business or as I like to think of them as the "Infrastructure Costs" of the business.

Basically, these are the costs relating to the infrastructure that you need to have in place to operate your business.

These costs are indirect costs as they are not directly related to the generation of sales, instead they relate to the facilities and operations you must have in place to run the business. Think of rent, rates, insurance, marketing, professional costs, sales and administration employees, and utilities.

These are the costs that exist regardless of the sales you make.

The Gross Profit (from Part 1 above) less the Overheads or Infrastructure costs produce the EBITDA, a key business metric.

EBITDA stands for:

- **E**arnings
- **B**efore
- **I**nterest
- **T**ax
- **D**epreciation, and
- **A**mortisation.

Understanding EBITDA is crucial for business growth as it provides insight into the operational profitability and cash flow generation capabilities of a business, independent of its capital structure. This knowledge can help in making informed decisions to drive success.

EBITDA focuses on the company's core trading performance and the profit generation from it. It is often used for comparison purposes between businesses and sale/exit prices are usually based on it.

It is effectively the ability of the business to generate cash from its operational trading business.

You must understand it.

Even more importantly, you must know how to measure it, calculate it, and influence it.

What do the individual parts mean?

Earnings – this is the profit generated from your trading business.

Before

Interest – the cost of borrowing money

Tax – Corporation Tax.

Depreciation – think of this as spreading the cost of a fixed asset over its useful productive life. For example, a van costing £20,000 with a useful life of 4 years – the annual depreciation charge is £5,000.

Amortisation – this is similar to depreciation, but it is a charge to write off goodwill over its useful life. Goodwill arises where you buy a business and you pay more than the net asset value of the company. It is the excess over the net asset value.

EBITDA is often the metric on which the exit value of businesses is based, and it is a key number that acquirers look at in detail. It shows the quality of your earnings.

Part 3: Retained Profit

Thereafter, the following items are categorised and accounted for:

- Interest
- Tax
- Depreciation
- Amortisation
- Profit After Tax
- Dividends*
- Retained Profit

*during the year this is usually accounted for by way of Directors' Loan Account, which is money the director owes the business. Once the dividend is declared and approved it offsets against the loan balance.

In preparing and reviewing Management Accounts I like to have prior year figures and budgeted figures as this allows trends to be identified, growth to be visible and again to drive or correct, and to improve performance.

If we do this based on information rather than "gut feel" then so much the better.

Balance Sheet

I likened the profit and loss account to a video covering a period of time. Think of the Balance Sheet or Statement of Financial position as a photograph at a point in time. It is a snapshot at a specific point in time, usually at month end or year end. However, in theory it can be established any day.

This statement lists all of the assets and liabilities in the business (top part) and how they are funded - equity (bottom part).

The top part must equal the bottom part, hence it "balances" and results in the "Balance Sheet" name.

Assets are listed in the order of liquidity from least liquid to most liquid.

Assets – these are things the company owns split into different categories:

- Fixed assets – long-term assets used in the running of the business and include buildings, equipment, vehicles, computers, and fixtures and fittings.

- Intangible assets – these are assets that we cannot physically see and include goodwill, patents, and trademarks.

- Current assets – those that can convert into cash within 12 months typically:
    - Stock – including work-in-progress (work done, but not yet invoiced)
    - Trade debtors – people who owe you money
    - Prepayments – items you have paid for, but not used, like rent in advance
    - Other debtors – other people who owe you money or assets
    - Director Loan Account – money that the director/s owes to the business
    - Bank
    - Cash

This gives the total Assets in the business.

Then we have the **Liabilities**.

Liabilities are what the company owes and are generally split between Current Liabilities – financial obligations due within 12 months and Long-term liabilities those due in more than a year.

- Current liabilities – those that need to be paid within 12 months typically:
    - Trade creditors – people you owe money to
    - Accruals – work done/materials received, but not yet invoiced to you
    - Other creditors – other people to whom you owe money
    - Director Loan Account – money that the business owes to the director/s

- - Hire Purchase/Bank Loans – the element due within 12 months
  - Bank overdraft
  - Amounts due to HM Revenue & Customs – PAYE/NIC, VAT, Corporation Tax
- Long-term liabilities - These normally comprise the 12 months plus element of loans and hire purchase.

A key figure I like to calculate is net current assets – this is the difference between current assets and current liabilities. Ideally, we want this to be positive. If it is negative, it usually indicates cash challenges and problems because it means the business is expected to pay more out within the next 12 months than is likely to turn into cash.

It is always a warning sign.

Do you know your net current assets position? It is a key figure to track.

In summary, the balance sheet provides an overview of your company's financial standing.

Although Net Asset Value shows the net figure – it is not the value of the business (see Chapter 12 Sale and Exit). It merely represents the excess of assets over liabilities unless there are more liabilities in which case your business would have a deficiency of net assets.

In theory, if you were to stop trading and sell all assets at the value shown and pay all of the liabilities then you would end up with the net asset value (less selling costs and taxation).

My two favourite, and key numbers for any business are Gross Margin and EBITDA.
Why?

It lets me understand the profitability and indicative value of any business.

If these are the only two numbers I am permitted to know about any business I can make a reasonably educated guess about the valuation and success of the business.

I have explained the importance of both above and I encourage you to monitor them closely – include them in your KPIs.

Real time information

In 1994, I learned a very valuable thing from the director in charge of the private equity company I was working for: "If you do everything every day, you are only ever a day behind."

It seems simple and obvious and is great advice.

This was in the days before online accounting and banking. However, it was still possible to arrange people, systems, and procedures to do just that. I applied this in my first role in industry and have continued to apply it in my career.

What does it mean in practice? Perform a daily bank reconciliation, issue sales invoices, post purchase invoices, update forecasts and other.

Remember my 3 daily questions that you must ask every day?

This is simple, and more importantly, very effective.

Remember, doing ordinary things well and regularly produces extraordinary results.

Example: "Meghan and Harry"

Do you know how much money you had in the bank last month? What about last week? Today? What about next week? Next month? Longer?

None of us has a crystal ball and as a result cannot be certain what will happen. However, we can make assumptions based on where we are and where we are going.

As I have said before, in my view, forecasting is the key to success alongside my 2 rules.

Let me tell you about "Meghan and Harry."

On wages day, Harry would be sitting at his desk and the phone would ring.

Meghan would call and ask, "Harry, how are we paying the wages today?"

Harry would typically respond, "I have no idea. Okay, we have 7 hours to fix it." This caused a lot of stress and Harry didn't always manage to pay everyone, and regularly didn't pay himself.

They implemented my weekly rolling cash flow forecast, and now, Harry has visibility of how he is paying the next 3 months of salaries with no more calls on wages day. What a difference! As Harry says, he no longer stresses over cash and sleeps much more soundly at night.

Staying Current

Most companies use online software – there are lots of options including Xero, QuickBooks, Free Agent, or Sage Online.

There are also various apps that integrate into these systems and free up lots of time and get information in quicker and with less administration.

There is no excuse for not having your financial information up-to-date.

Do everything every day. Focus on the right numbers. It works.

Composition of Management Accounts

Let's break down the components of management accounts:

- Profit and Loss (P&L) Account: Shows revenues, costs, and expenses during a specific period. It's your primary tool for gauging profitability. Think of it as a video or film of your operations.

- Balance Sheet: Offers a snapshot of assets, liabilities, and equity at a specific point in time. It tells you what your business owns and owes. Think of it as a photo of your business at a point in time.

- Cash Flow Statement: Tracks the flow of cash in and out of your business, highlighting your operational, investing, and financing activities.

Regularity and Timeliness

How often should you review these accounts? Monthly is typical, but the more frequent, the better. Timely insights allow you to react swiftly to business and market changes, adjust your strategies, seize opportunities as they arise, and deal with threats.

Analysing Management Accounts

To truly leverage these tools:

- P&L Analysis: Look beyond the bottom line. Analyse trends in sales, costs, and profitability.

- Balance Sheet Examination: Review and understand all assets and liabilities. Consider liquidity and solvency.

- Cash Flow Scrutiny: Ensure your operations generate enough cash to sustain and grow your business.

Operational Insights from Management Accounts

Management accounts illuminate paths to operational efficiency. They can reveal cost overruns, underutilised assets, or unexpectedly profitable or loss-making areas, guiding you to make adjustments that improve the bottom line.

KPIs and Management Accounts

Key Performance Indicators (KPIs) should emerge naturally from your management accounts. Common KPIs include gross profit margin, net profit margin, utilisation, charge out rate, and debtor days. Choose KPIs that align closely with your business goals and monitor them consistently.

Utilising Management Accounts for Growth

These financial tools are not just for troubleshooting—they're also for scaling. Use the insights gained from your management accounts to support expansion plans, justify capital investments, or prepare for fundraising.

Management Accounts and Stakeholder Communication

Clear, concise management accounts can boost your credibility with stakeholders. They serve as evidence of your business acumen and your company's stability or growth potential, which is invaluable in negotiations with investors, banks, and partners.

Critical Points

- Navigating the Financial Landscape: Explore the role of management accounts in understanding the current financial position.

- Financial Wizardry: Find someone to simplify the concept of financial management, making it accessible to you, the business owner.
- Take Charge of Your Destiny: I want to empower readers to use management accounts as a tool for steering their businesses forward effectively.

Conclusion

Embracing management accounts gives you a profound command over your business' direction. With these tools, you are not just running your business day-to-day; you are steering it towards long-term success.

If you haven't set up your management accounting system yet, now's the time. Start simple, focus on regular updates, and use the data to drive decisions. Here's a checklist to get you started:

- Monthly P&L account and balance sheet updates
- Regular review of trade debtors, trade creditors, stock, and work in progress
- Weekly cash flow forecasts

Frequently Asked Questions

Question: What are the critical components of management accounts that you believe every business owner should focus on?

Answer: The critical components of management accounts include timely and accurate financial data, comprehensive profit and loss account (income statement), balance sheets, cash flow statements, and variance analysis. Reviewing these components monthly allows business owners to make informed decisions, identify trends, and address issues promptly. Additionally, including Key Performance Indicators (KPIs) in management accounts helps track the business' financial health and operational efficiency.

Question: How often should businesses review their management accounts?

Answer: Businesses should review their management accounts monthly to ensure they have a clear understanding of their financial position. Regular reviews enable timely adjustments and strategic planning. KPIs should be reviewed more frequently, with some being monitored weekly or even daily, to maintain a close watch on critical aspects of the business's performance. They let you know if you've had a good day, good week and a good month.

Question: What are the most critical mistakes businesses make with their management accounts?

Answer: Common mistakes businesses make with their management accounts include delays in preparation, neglecting to update stock and work-in-progress (WIP) figures, and improperly recording accruals and prepayments (see Glossary at Appendix 1). These errors can lead to inaccurate financial reporting and misinformed decision-making. Ensuring timely and accurate updates to all components of management accounts is essential for maintaining financial integrity.

Question: How often should management accounts be reviewed for optimal impact?

Answer: For optimal impact, management accounts should be reviewed in detail monthly. This review should include variance analysis to compare actual performance against budgets and forecasts. Understanding the reasons behind variances helps management make informed decisions and necessary adjustments to stay on track with their financial goals.

Key Takeaways
- Regular review and analysis are key to leveraging these tools for business success.
- Align your KPIs with business objectives for targeted performance monitoring.

Action Items
- Prepare monthly Management Accounts in your business.
- Learn and understand some key metrics including Gross Margin and EBITDA.
- Be aware of the layout of a profit and loss account, and a balance sheet.

Know Your Numbers

NOTES

Chapter 5: Actual versus Budget Variance Analysis

NOTES

This chapter links closely to Chapter 10 on Forecasts. Without a budget or a forecast then there can be no variance analysis.

What is a variance?

Quite simply a variance is the difference between a budgeted or forecast outcome and the actual outcome.

I like to look at overall variances and the variances on a line-by-line basis especially in the profit and loss account or income statement.

I am a huge fan of Actual versus Budget and Variance Analysis. I believe that it drives performance. Quite simply if it is a good variance, understand it, and do more of it. If it is a bad variance, understand it and, do less of it by making changes.

This part is so important. Why?

It gives a much better understanding of what we thought or anticipated was going to happen (from our budget or forecast) and what actually happened.

Why was the outcome different from that which we forecast?

There can be various reasons for the variances. These include:

- Poor performance
- Poor budgeting or forecasting as a result of incorrect assumptions
- Change in circumstances
- Changes in price
- Changes in the work or project
- Delays or movements in timescales

We need to understand the reasons and we need to understand whether the variance is a one-off or something that fundamentally or substantially changes things going forward.

If it does, we need to understand the impact on our forecasting.

We use the variance analysis to make changes, to make better decisions and to run the business. If we simply ignore the variances, we learn nothing, make no changes, and continue to run the business in blissful ignorance.

Variance analysis is a key tool in driving performance.
I like to have the management accounts (and in particular the profit and loss account) prepared showing the monthly results, the year-to-date results and also the budget for the month and year-to-date, alongside the monthly variance and the year-to-date variance.

Then I like to review it on a line-by-line basis and understand the different variances.

- Is it good or bad?
- Do I want to do more of it?
- Or, do I want to do less of it?
- Why has it arisen?

I need to understand all of that before I decide what to do and what impact it has on the business.

I like to run the business using the forecast and the variance analysis.

You can learn so much about performance and what is happening in the business.

The danger of only doing it in totality is that you may miss variances within service lines or product lines or for particular customers.

For example, the total gross profit for the month and year to date may be ahead of budget. What do we do? Pat ourselves on the back and move on? No. I want to see it broken down by service line or product or project. Some may be ahead of budget. Great – do more of it. However, some may be behind budget and by taking an overall approach we may miss the individual variances and the opportunity to learn and make changes at a detailed level. That is how you use the information to make better decisions and drive performance.

Remember. Variance analysis gives you better information to allow you to make better decisions and to make changes. It keeps people and departments accountable and drives performance. By analysing the figures in a detailed manner, we can identify issues and opportunities that we would otherwise miss. It gives us the opportunity to understand and make changes or indeed do more of what is working. If we do this monthly it gives us regular and quick feedback, thereby allowing changes and understanding how it impacts on going forward.

In summary, variance analysis provides two key benefits:

1. Valuable insights into operational performance from a financial perspective
2. It promotes accountability and helps decision making.

Simple.

It is important that it is done monthly and, ideally, as soon as possible because it allows changes to be made and the opportunity to change and influence the current month. Leave it too late and that opportunity has gone.

One other thing to remember. If you don't have a budget or a forecast, then you cannot perform variance analysis!

As I will stress more in Chapter 10, I believe that there is only one way to run a business without a forecast or a budget. That is badly!

Remember the plane and the dashboard?

This is a key part of your dashboard. Embrace it and you will see a significant change in performance and also your forecasting abilities.

Critical Points

- Clarity, Certainty and Visibility: Learn how to perform a comparison of actual performance against budget to provide clarity, certainty and visibility for decision-making.

- Seizing Control Every Day: I encourage daily engagement with financials to maintain control over your business and its trajectory.

- Interactive Elements: My goal is to pose questions to engage readers in reflecting on their own actual versus budget assessments.

Conclusion

Variance analysis is not just a retrospective tool but a forward-looking compass that guides your strategic decisions. By regularly comparing actual performance against your forecast or budget, you can maintain control over your business trajectory and adjust course as needed for success.

Start today by reviewing your last month's performance against your budget. Identify one area of significant variance, investigate its causes, and decide on an appropriate action. Regular engagement with your financials is the key to proactive management.

Frequently Asked Questions

Question: What are the most important aspects of variance analysis that businesses often overlook?

Answer: One of the most critical aspects of variance analysis that businesses often overlook is the importance of having a budget or forecast in the first place. Without these, it's impossible to perform variance analysis. Additionally, some businesses neglect to regularly conduct variance analysis, missing out on valuable insights that can help them adjust their strategies and improve performance.

Question: Can you provide an example of how variance analysis helped a business correct its course?

Answer: Variance analysis can be instrumental in identifying discrepancies such as sales shortfalls, margin shortfalls, and overheads running ahead of budget. For example, a business might notice that its actual sales are significantly lower than forecast. By investigating the cause, it may find issues like decreased customer demand or ineffective marketing strategies. Addressing these issues can help the business get back on track and improve its overall performance.

Question: How can businesses set realistic budgets that are flexible yet effective?

Answer: Understand where you are and where you have been. Take these assumptions and use them to understand where you are going. A forecast is just a series of assumptions. To set realistic and flexible budgets, businesses should start by understanding their current financial position and historical performance. These insights help create informed assumptions about future performance. A well-constructed forecast is essentially a series of these assumptions, which should be regularly reviewed and adjusted based on actual results and changing conditions.

Question: What role does technology play in enhancing the effectiveness of variance analysis?

Answer: While technology can assist in automating some aspects of variance analysis, such as data collection and report generation, the process still requires significant manual input. Financial software like Xero, QuickBooks, and Castaway can help streamline data management and reporting, but the interpretation and adjustment based on variance analysis are typically manual tasks that require a thorough understanding of the business.

Action Items

- Understand how variance analysis can improve your business performance.
- Perform monthly variance analysis in your business.
- Make changes to your business based on findings from variance analysis.

Chapter 6: Key Performance Indicators ("KPIs")

NOTES

How do you know you've had a good day, week, or month?

This is a question I always pose to a business owner when we first meet.

It is usually met with a few different responses:

- I don't know and never know until the end of the month (or in some cases end of the year)
- All of my people/vehicles have been on-site
- The phones/website have been really busy

Okay, that's great. However, I want you to prove it financially not by how you feel or instinct. Can you point to how you measure it? Can you tell me what that means financially? Almost 100% of the time the response to both questions is "no". If that is you, too, then I want to change that for you.

KPI stands for Key Performance Indicator. Let's break that down:

- **Key** – of crucial or essential importance
- **Performance** - the execution or accomplishment of a task, action, or activity
- **Indicator** - a measurement or value which gives you an idea of what something is like

We can use KPIs to focus on key areas of importance relating to different activities or actions and have a measurement for them.

Does that make sense?

Remember the first word. Key.

We do not need 20 or 30 KPIs – in that case, they are performance indicators rather than key performance indicators. Pick between 3 and 6 things that determine the success of your trading performance and that you can monitor, manage, and influence. We can use KPIs on a daily, weekly, monthly, or annual basis. Whilst KPIs are useful, they tell you after the fact and are not predictive. However, you can see trends. You can see how things are moving.

They can provide an early warning of problems or indeed opportunities, and allow you to see what is happening in your business and how it is performing before month end. They can also allow you to face reality and understand what needs to change and/or improve. It is great if you have a standard to compare it against. Perhaps an industry figure, a competitor of something that you are driving towards.

KPIs allow you to measure and monitor trends, but you must understand them. What do they mean? What is the impact on the future?

You must measure the right things and that is why I like between 3 and 6 KPIs.

The frequency of measurement – daily/weekly/monthly – will be determined by the metric and the ease in which it can be measured.

- What is the standard?
- What needs to change?
- What needs to improve?

The key is to prioritise – what will drive profits and cash flow?

We can use the information to manage uncertainty and we can measure them to drive performance. KPIs can highlight gaps/weaknesses/problems.

In summary, KPIs are quantifiable measures of performance over time for a specific objective. KPIs provide targets for teams to aim for, milestones to gauge progress, and insights that help people throughout the company make better decisions. It allows you to compare against prior periods and also against industry metrics/averages.

KPIs are the key targets you should track to make the most impact on your strategic business outcomes. KPIs support your strategy and help your teams focus on what's important. They provide a health check and give a realistic indication of the health of the company and its trading performance, and allow you to hold your teams accountable.

Types of KPIs

There are many different categories of KPIs. While some are used to measure monthly progress against a goal, others can have a longer-term focus. They include:

- Financial
- Strategic
- Operational performance
- Sales
- Marketing
- Divisional

The tendency can be to manage the things that are easy.

I approach it differently.

I want to manage the ones that drive profit and cash as that is the key to a successful business.

My favourite KPIs are:
- Gross Margin – the Gross Profit as a percentage of sales (ideally by product/service line/project)
- EBITDA
- Cash
- Trade Debtor Days – how many days sales are tied up
- Stock/WIP days – how many days sales are tied up
- Utilisation
- Average charge out rate
- Product profit / service line profit

Remember when developing KPIs, it is tempting to measure everything and/or the easy things. Don't. Focus on what will allow you to answer the question: **"How do you know you have had a good day/week/month?"**

Then you won't go far wrong.

You also need to understand how you will use them and how often, how they are calculated and who is evaluated on the outcomes of them.

For example, we could manage the operational team based on gross margin; the sales team on orders; and the credit control team on debtor days. Work out what is important to you for each area of your business and what you can influence.

Whatever you do though, make them clear and avoid having too many.

Manage, monitor, and change if required – quickly. Time is of the essence.

Use KPIs in the decision-making process and to improve performance. Don't just measure for the sake of it. Measure what is important.

And measure what you can control, influence, and improve.

Example: Dragons' Den
We all have seen Dragons' Den.

Who is your favourite Dragon?

Mine is Deborah. She's made a lot of money over the years and "knows her stuff."

In particular, she knows her numbers and wants to ensure that any company she invests in knows their numbers.

What usually happens in the den is that the pitch is going great, and there is lots of interest. Then Deborah asks, "Tell me about your numbers", and it all changes.

Why? They don't Know Their Numbers.

Of the approximate 1,000 Dragons' Den pitches, around 20% have received offers. However, around half of the deals were never actually completed, principally because the numbers didn't stand up to the financial due diligence.

You must Know Your Numbers. It's your business. There is no excuse. Please trust me; it's easy. Others who have worked with me agree.

Critical Points
- The Crux: Know Your Numbers: Learn more about the concept of KPIs as essential tools for measuring current business health.

- Key Daily Questions for Financial Mastery: Propose and ask yourself daily questions regarding KPIs to ensure effective cash management.

- The Power of Education: Understand the transformative effect of educating yourself, as the business owner, on KPIs and their financial implications.

Conclusion

KPIs are not just numbers—they are a reflection of your business strategy in action. By effectively selecting, monitoring, and responding to KPIs, you can enhance your operational focus, improve strategic outcomes, and drive competitive advantage.

Review your current set of KPIs. Are they aligned with your strategic goals? Are they providing the insights you need to make informed decisions? Challenge yourself to refine or expand your KPIs to better meet your business objectives.

Frequently Asked Questions

Question: What are some KPIs you consider essential that haven't been covered in detail?

Answer: Essential KPIs include gross margin, EBITDA (Earnings Before Interest, Taxes, Depreciation, and Amortisation), cash balance, debtor days (the average number of days it takes to collect receivables), sales utilisation, and average charge-out rates. These KPIs provide critical insights into a business's profitability, liquidity, efficiency, and overall financial health.

Question: How should businesses set and adjust their KPIs over time?

Answer: Monitor, manage, and review in line with variance analysis. Businesses should set KPIs based on their strategic objectives and regularly review them in conjunction with variance analysis. This process helps ensure that KPIs remain relevant and aligned with the business's goals. As conditions change, businesses should adjust their KPIs to reflect new priorities and market realities. KPIs need to be things that can be monitored, measured, and influenced to drive performance.

Question: How should businesses communicate and implement KPI tracking across different departments?

Answer: Effective communication and implementation of KPI tracking involve assigning responsibility to divisional heads for achieving agreed budgets and KPI targets. This approach ensures accountability and encourages each department to align their activities with the overall business objectives. Regular meetings and reporting help maintain focus and drive continuous improvement. Those responsible should be involved in agreeing upon the most effective KPIs.

Question: What are some innovative KPIs that businesses might not be aware of but should consider?

Answer: While traditional KPIs such as gross margin and cash flow are well-known, businesses can also consider innovative KPIs tailored to their specific industry or business model. Examples might include customer lifetime value (CLV), employee engagement scores, or digital marketing metrics like cost per acquisition (CPA). These KPIs can provide unique insights and drive strategic decision-making.

Action Items
- Understand what a Key performance Indicator is.
- Identify and create between 3 and 6 KPIs for your business.
- Monitor, manage and make changes based on your KPIs.

NOTES

SECTION 3 - WHERE HAVE YOU BEEN?

This is the shortest section in the book and is included for completeness rather than providing lots of new information, guidance, and tips.

Why?

I don't like looking back. I want businesses to focus on looking forward. We cannot change the past and what has happened, but we can learn from it. We can understand what has happened and make assumptions with respect to what is likely to happen based on what has happened. This allows us to better understand the future.

It is important as it provides a lot of information that we can use and learn from. Remember, better decisions come from better information. Use this information and move on.

NOTES

Chapter 7: Prior Years

NOTES

How many times have you sat with your spouse or partner on a Friday evening and said, "why don't we go shopping for car tyres at the weekend." I expect never.

Statutory accounts filed at Companies House are a bit like that.

We do it because we have to legally and they are a commodity item.

Nobody likes preparing them.

Nobody likes paying for them.

They add very little value.

However, just like your car needs legal tyres, statutory accounts need to be filed to preserve limited liability.

They are also useful for suppliers who typically credit check you before offering credit terms so the better your financial position looks then the higher the credit limit and better terms you are likely to be able to negotiate.

I encourage my growing profitable clients to file their accounts as early as possible for two reasons. Firstly, it is good practice and secondly it allows credit limits to change quicker.

Yes, we have 9 months to file the accounts, but why wait?

We can't change what has happened.

File and move on.

If you have had a bad year or you want to maintain confidentiality for longer, then these are justifiable reasons for waiting until closer to the deadline.

I filed my last year end accounts within 9 days of year end – it should have been 6, but I had to move the meeting with my accountant from Friday until Monday!

What are Statutory Accounts?

These are the accounts that you must file annually at Companies House in order to preserve the limited liability of the company.

They are filed 9 months after year end and follow a legal framework as set out in the Companies Act and related accounting standards.

Typically, your external accountant will prepare these for you based on your management accounts and accounting software.

Smaller companies, as defined in the rules, have certain exemptions and are able to file summarised versions and show less detail than large companies.

Your company is defined as 'small' if it has any 2 of the following:

- turnover of £10.2 million or less
- £5.1 million or less on its balance sheet
- 50 employees or less

Please note that the government has indicated it will introduce legislation to change these thresholds, so please check before making any decisions based on this. There are also imminent changes through secondary legislation issued as part of the Economic Crime and Corporate Transparency Act 2023 which is currently awaited. This will see the small company turnover threshold increase to £15m and balance sheet of £7.5m.

If your company is small, you can:

- use the exemption so your company's accounts do not need to be audited
- choose whether or not to send a copy of the director's report and profit and loss account to Companies House
- send abridged/filleted accounts to Companies House (all members must agree)

What are audited accounts?

An audit must be performed by a registered auditor (usually an accountancy firm) and must comply with certain accounting standards. It involves performing procedures on the numbers disclosed in the financial statements, and these procedures are designed to identify material misstatements and usually involve testing a sample of transactions and balances. It refers to materiality and it doesn't necessarily mean that everything is 100% correct.

On the basis that the focus of this book is on companies typically below the audit threshold, that should suffice.

Statutory accounts are not particularly useful in terms of running the business. They have a compliance focus rather than a focus on information for making decisions and evaluating performance.

What are management accounts?

That is why we prepare management accounts – the name derives from the accounts for management purposes – allowing us to run the business better and make better decisions.

As I stated at the start of this section and chapter, I don't like looking back. We can't change anything that has happened, but we can learn from it. It is also important that we comply with legislation and keep our business right. My advice – do that, do it quickly, and move on.

Conclusion

The past is a powerful indicator of potential future outcomes. By rigorously analysing prior years' financial data, you can make more informed decisions that not only avoid past pitfalls but also build on proven successes.

Dive into your business' financial history. Start with the last three to five years and conduct a thorough review. What trends do you see? What lessons can be learned? Schedule regular reviews to keep this historical perspective fresh and relevant.

Frequently Asked Questions

Question: What specific benefits have you seen businesses gain from analysing data from previous years?

Answer: Analysing data from previous years helps businesses gain a better understanding of their trading patterns and key assumptions. This historical perspective allows businesses to identify trends, evaluate the effectiveness of past strategies, and make more informed decisions for the future. By learning from past successes and mistakes, businesses can improve their forecasting and strategic planning.

Question: Are there tools or methods you recommend for conducting this analysis?

Answer: Conducting an analytical review of prior periods, years, and months is a straightforward yet effective method for analysing historical data. Tools like spreadsheets, financial software, and data visualisation platforms can help organise and present this data in a meaningful way. Regularly comparing past performance metrics against current data helps identify patterns and areas for improvement.

Question: How can businesses effectively use historical data to forecast future performance?

Answer: To effectively use historical data for forecasting, businesses need to understand what has happened in the past and the key assumptions that influenced those outcomes. By identifying recurring trends and factors that impacted performance, businesses can make more accurate predictions about future performance. Historical data provides a foundation for creating realistic and data-driven forecasts.

Question: What specific financial indicators should businesses focus on from previous years?

Answer: Businesses should focus on identifying trends and changes in key financial indicators from previous years. These indicators include revenue growth, profit margins, cash flow, and expenses. By analysing how these metrics have evolved over time, businesses can gain insights into their financial stability, growth potential, and areas that may require attention.

Key Takeaways

- Historical financial analysis is crucial for understanding business trends and informing future strategies.

- Regular reviews of past financial data can prevent repeated mistakes and highlight successful strategies for further development.

Action Items
- Understand the format of statutory accounts and the filing rules.
- Have your prior year information prepared within a month of year end.
- Identify trends in your annual performance.

Chapter 8: Compliance

NOTES

Compliance refers to the various filings we need to make whether accounts, taxation, employee information or legislation in general.

There are various things that as business owners we need to do, and it is important that we do them and within the correct time scales.

These include various items below. Please note that this is not an exhaustive list, but for high level information only. I am not a compliance expert and outsource all of my compliance related matters.

Companies House and HM Revenue & Customs:
- Statutory accounts as discussed above
- Corporation tax return (see section 9 below)
- Confirmation Statement annual filing at Companies House showing directors, shareholders, and registered office details.
- VAT

Employee Returns
- PAYE
- National Insurance

Regulatory Compliance
From a wider company law perspective we also need to address and comply with legislation including:

- Employment Law
- Data Protection
- Health & Safety

You may also be subject to certain industry standards, laws, and accreditations. It is vital to operate within these and keep up-to-date.

Like all of these things, I encourage the use of specialists who know what they are doing.

I do not enjoy compliance and have no expertise in the area so I will leave it at that.

Action Items

- Funders' Expectations: You must have a clear understanding of past compliance and taxation positions businesses for successful funding opportunities and growth.

- Know the tax liability – plan and prepare.

- Understand the impact of up-to-date accounts on credit limits.

Conclusion

Effective compliance is not just about avoiding penalties—it's about building a business that is sustainable, ethical, and prepared for long-term success. A robust compliance program not only protects against risks but also enhances business reputation and stakeholder confidence.

Evaluate your current compliance practices. Are there gaps that need addressing? Implement a compliance calendar to keep track of necessary updates and training, ensuring your business remains compliant and ahead of potential risks.

Frequently Asked Questions

Question: What are common compliance issues that you've seen in businesses?

Answer: Common compliance issues in businesses include failing to adhere to regulatory requirements and leaving compliance tasks until the last minute. These issues can lead to penalties, legal complications, and damage to the business's reputation. In severe circusmatnces they may lead to a cessation of trading. To avoid these problems, businesses should establish clear compliance procedures and stay up-to-date with regulatory changes.

Question: How do you suggest businesses stay updated with compliance requirements?

Answer: Having a good accountant is crucial for staying updated with financial compliance requirements. Accountants can provide valuable guidance on regulatory changes and ensure that the business adheres to all relevant accounting laws and standards. Additionally, businesses should invest in continuous education and training for their staff to keep them informed about compliance obligations for their sector and engage appropriate legal and other specialist advisers including employee and human resources, health and safety and industry experts.

Question: What strategies do you recommend for small businesses to improve their compliance processes?

Answer: Small businesses can improve their compliance processes by implementing daily routines and timely filing of required documents. Establishing a systematic approach to compliance tasks, such as maintaining accurate records and conducting regular audits, helps ensure that nothing is overlooked. Utilising compliance management software can also streamline the process and reduce the risk of errors.

Question: Can you provide examples of how compliance issues have impacted businesses and how they recovered?

Answer: Compliance issues, such as not being aware of corporation tax liabilities until the last minute, can create panic and cash flow problems for businesses. However, businesses can recover by proactively addressing these issues. For example, by completing year-end accounts quickly and calculating corporation tax early, businesses can build tax payments into their cash flow forecasts and avoid last-minute surprises. Implementing a proactive approach to compliance helps maintain financial stability and reduces stress.

Action Items
- Ensure all compliance filings are up-to-date.
- Be aware of your corporation tax liability and when it is due for payment.
- Ensure the corporation tax amount due is included in your forecast.

Chapter 9: Taxation

NOTES

Like the previous section on Compliance, I caveat this section on the basis that I am not a tax expert.

I have my own accountant who deals with all of my corporate and related taxes and I encourage all of my clients to do so too.

I believe in using specialists in your business and focusing on your area of expertise. Surround yourself with the right people.

Tax is a specialist area and should be left to the specialists.

As a result, this section is again only for awareness and high-level information.

I stated above that the reason I like the yearend/statutory accounts to be prepared quickly is that it allows the Corporation Tax return to be completed and therefore we know our tax liability.

Corporation Tax Rates

The Corporation Tax liability must be paid 9 months and 1 day after the company year end.

By knowing the amount due, we can plan and include it in our forecast.

The main rate of corporation tax is 25% for the financial year beginning 1 April 2023 (previously 19% in the financial year beginning 1 April 2022). This can change annually depending on what the government decide at "the Budget" so be sure to check it.

At present, the main 25% rate applies to companies with profits in excess of £250.000. There is a "small company rate" which is 19% and applies to profits below £50,000.

For those companies with profits in the £50,000 to £250,000 range there is a sliding scale of tax rates.

There are lots of other rules and regulations that fall outside the scope of this book, and which are unlikely to impact most smaller companies. I will add employee/employment taxes to that too.

As stated, I encourage you to take specialist tax advice – a good tax advisor can save you and your business a lot of money.

Conclusion

Effective tax management is not merely a compliance requirement but a strategic component of overall business management. By understanding and actively managing your tax obligations, you can protect your business from risks and capitalise on opportunities to reduce tax liabilities.

Review your tax strategies and ensure they align with the current laws and your business goals. Consider consulting with a tax professional to optimise your planning and compliance.

Frequently Asked Questions

Question: What are the most challenging aspects of taxation for SMEs?

Answer: While taxation can be challenging for small and medium-sized enterprises (SMEs), these challenges can be mitigated by working with a good accountant and tax advisor. The most common issues arise from leaving tax planning until the last minute and failing to forecast tax payments. By engaging with professionals and planning ahead, SMEs can manage their tax obligations more effectively.

Question: Can you provide tips or strategies for effective tax planning?

Answer: Do it quickly. Effective tax planning requires prompt action and foresight. Businesses should regularly review their financial performance and consult with tax advisors to identify potential liabilities and opportunities for tax savings. By staying proactive and addressing tax matters early, businesses can minimise their tax burden and avoid last-minute surprises.

Question: What are some common tax-related mistakes made by small businesses?

Answer: A common tax-related mistake made by small businesses is filing (and paying) their taxes late. This can result in penalties, interest charges, and added stress. To avoid these issues, businesses should establish a clear timeline for tax preparation and filing, ensuring that all necessary documents are submitted on time.

Question: How should businesses approach tax planning at different stages of their growth?

Answer: Forecast it. At different stages of growth, businesses should approach tax planning with a focus on forecasting. During the startup phase, businesses should project their tax liabilities based on expected revenues and expenses. As the business grows, it should regularly update these forecasts to reflect changes in its financial situation. By integrating tax planning into their overall financial strategy, businesses can manage their tax obligations more effectively and plan for future growth. The accountant can provide a quarterly update of the current year taxes and ideally do it monthly as part of the management accounts process.

Action Items
- Understand the different tax rates.

- Engage a good tax accountant.

- Arrange your affairs is the most tax efficient way with effective planning.

NOTES

NOTES

SECTION 4 - WHERE ARE YOU GOING

This is my favourite section and where I spend most time with my clients.

"If you don't know where you are going, any road will take you there."

A phrase attributed to Lewis Carroll. It didn't actually appear that way in the Alice in Wonderland Books, although that sentiment was precisely what the discussion between Alice and the Cat was about.

It is a bit like running a business.

I wrote an article for Daily Business a few years ago. "Good Planning Will Work Wonders on Your Business' Prospects."

It focused on the importance of having a financial map for your business and that without it you will struggle for direction.

Remember that throughout this section.

NOTES

Chapter 10: Forecasts

NOTES

The future is uncertain.
We do not have a crystal ball.

We do not know what is going to happen.

However, we can make educated guesses or estimates on what may happen based on what we know today and what we know has happened previously.

Think about the weather.
We know that Glasgow is not renowned for lots of sunshine and that from, let's say, November through to February, it will probably be cold and wet.

If we are in December then we can expect, or forecast, a cold and wet day.

How do we make that forecast?
Quite simply by using the best information available to us.

Based on where we are (Glasgow in December) and based on historic evidence (cold and wet between November and February) of what has happened previously.

Let's apply that to your business and its financial information.

What then is a budget or a forecast?
It is basically a series of assumptions based on the best information we have available today.

Those assumptions may change tomorrow, so our forecast needs to be dynamic and regularly updated for these changes in assumptions and actual results.

I could keep this chapter very short and simple and stop here!

In general, people are scared of forecasting.
It makes us uncomfortable because of the uncertainty and the potential to get things wrong.

Let's make it a little easier.

Work on the basis that your forecast will be wrong, as it probably will.

However, by preparing it, you take an element of the uncertainty away because you are thinking about it and what may happen based on where you are and what has happened previously.

Just like the weather forecast above.

Where to start
Many business owners do not know where to start when it comes to forecasting.

The best thing to do is to start!

Few of us are trained in weather forecasting, but we can make an educated guess on what the weather may be based on the best information available.

From a business forecasting perspective just make a start.

Trust me, your first stab at a forecast can't be as bad as operating blind without a forecast.

Like anything, the more you do something, the better you become at it.

If you don't understand financial statements, it makes forecasting even more challenging.

By reading this book, you have given yourself another advantage.

You now have a much better understanding of financial statements and your numbers.

That is why in Know Your Numbers, we start with "Where Are You" and then "Where Have You Been" as it provides context and gives a starting point.

It explains your numbers in a way that you can understand them.

Think of your forecast as a map for your journey
Forecasting is quite simply predicting what will happen in the future by taking into consideration events in the past and present.

It allows us to deal with uncertainty by creating an element of certainty.

We use information and trends, alongside where we are today.

Simple as that.

Don't turn it into something it is not.

Take away the fear.

I work on the basis that most forecasts will be wrong
That's fine.

It is not an exercise in precision.

It is a guide telling us where we are aiming to go and what resources we need.

That is why it needs to be updated regularly.

It is why I focus so much on Actual versus Budget Variance Analysis with my clients, and is why what we discussed in Chapter 5 is so important.

We must keep reviewing and changing our forecast by using the best information we have.

When I say regularly, typically for the monthly forecasts I like to update it monthly, and for the weekly forecasts to update weekly.

The key aim of a budget or forecast is to provide clarity, certainty, and visibility of where you are going, and to show the resources required – usually people and cash.

Budgeting versus Forecasting

While budgets are usually made for an entire year, forecasts are usually updated more regularly, in my view monthly works well. Through forecasting, a company can project where it's going, and it may adjust its direction based on what the updated forecast shows.

Remember, budgeting and forecasting refers to the practice of predicting what will happen in the future by taking into consideration events in the past and present.

While related, budgets and forecasts are separate concepts: a budget is a plan for a company's future, whereas a forecast is a sign of where the company is going. Based on the forecast, a budget may be altered to better reflect reality.

Forecasts help you focus on where you want to be and how you are going to get there. They give you a way to track and adjust your progress towards your business goals. With a forecast and regular tracking in place, your business will perform significantly better. You will also have clarity, certainty and visibility.

Forecasting helps with accountability, measurement and ownership or performance. If the wider team and/or departments are involved in the process it improves their buy-in and makes them feel part of the process. It becomes their budget rather than something imposed on them.

As stated at the beginning of this chapter, we don't have a crystal ball and don't know what is going to happen, but we can make assumptions.

A forecast is a series of assumptions and should be based on best information available at the time.

There could be 2 assumptions, there could be 102 assumptions or more.

If you review the assumptions and agree them on a line-by-line basis, then by default your forecast is correct.

Simple!

However, as I stated, you must adapt and change the forecast as new information becomes available. It must be dynamic.

All of my clients prepare a budget before the start of each financial year. Then, we update it monthly with actual results and keep updating it going forward. This means we have a budget and an updated forecast.

That is the terminology I like to use, whether it is right or wrong. It's how I think of it.

Why prepare a forecast?
There are many reasons including:

1. It is a map and target for going forward.
2. It shows the funding and other resources required.
3. We can use it for accountability. We want our various teams involved in the process, so we have their buy in – it is their budget too, not one that has been imposed on them.
4. We use it to measure performance – the regular actual versus budget variance analysis.

5. We use it to drive performance. We push to reach the targets we have set, rather than operating aimlessly.

Remember, use your forecast as a map for your journey.

What is the starting point of a forecast?
- Where you are and where you have been.

- Where you are is the starting position and is shown by your management accounts.

- Where you have been – use prior information to drive assumptions based on what has happened in your prior year accounts and financial information.

- Where you are going – use your assumptions and other things like order book, contracts, recurring revenue, work in progress and income expectations.

Costs are usually easier to forecast because you know what you have in place:

- Salaries – you know the people costs.

- Infrastructure costs – rent, rates, insurance.

Sales are harder, and can be impacted by seasonality. However, if you look at where you have been that will help.

I like to use two approaches:
- **Top down** – high level targets – we turned over £3.5 million last year – let's aim for £5 million this year.

- **Bottom up** – prepare a detailed analysis by customer/product/service/project and what you know.

Compare the two and ideally, they are close.

Remember, there is no right and wrong here.

It is your forecast and what you think might happen.

The forecast should comprise the profit and loss account, balance sheet, and cash flow on a monthly basis and cover at least the next full financial year, sometimes longer. This allows us to establish the funding required and can be shared with funders (see Chapter 11).

I also like to operate with a weekly rolling cash flow forecast (for a minimum of 13 weeks) either using an Excel workbook (you can download a version here: kynmastery.com/kyn-book-resources) or using an app like Float which integrates with your accounting software (it works on a monthly basis).

Again, this is not an exact science, but an attempt to provide certainty, mitigate risk, and reduce stress.

If will show where the "pinch" points are and where cash becomes tight or challenging. It also allows time to do something about it – bring receipts forward, defer outflows and/or secure more funding.

That is the whole point of this weekly forecast.

It is not about precision.

It is about creating clarity, certainty, and visibility.

It is about making sure you have time to react and do something about shortfalls.

Simple!

Example: "Elon"

Let's talk about "Elon" and what he calls his 'therapy' and how he is massively growing his business and cutting stress.

As I have said, my role is often that of a social worker, guidance counsellor and doctor.

Elon calls me his financial therapist. I tell clients to call me when they're stressed or lonely or if they just want to vent.

He does that, and he has also incorporated the Know Your Numbers framework in his business. He knows where he is, where he has been, and where he is going, and has a properly financed business to meet that growth.

He has gone from less than half a million and "on the tools" to an order book over £2M.

My clients always know that I am only a phone call away.

Always remember Alice and the Cat:
"If you don't know where you are going, any road will take you there."

Don't be a hostage to fortune and run your business blind.

Have a map for your journey.

Critical Points
- The Crystal Ball Conundrum: Remember the necessity of forecasting for business planning and avoiding chaotic financial management.

- The Forecasting Imperative: Without forecasts, businesses are essentially running blindly and inefficiently.

- The Game-Changer: The concept of a weekly rolling cash flow forecast can have a transformative effect on businesses like Megan and Harry's.

Conclusion
Effective forecasting is crucial for navigating the complexities of the business environment. It enables

organisations to be proactive rather than reactive, making informed decisions that drive growth and stability.

Review your organisation's forecasting capabilities. Are there areas where you can improve accuracy or efficiency? Consider engaging with forecasting experts or investing in new technologies to enhance your forecasting processes.

Frequently Asked Questions

Question: What forecasting methods do you find most effective?

Answer: Effective forecasting methods include creating an annual budget and updating its monthly based on actual performance, variance analysis, and changes both in the business environment and within the business. By regularly revising forecasts to account for new contracts, lost contracts, supplier price changes, and market fluctuations, businesses can ensure their financial plans remain accurate and relevant. Uptake assumptions change and new information becomes available.

Question: How can businesses better integrate forecasting into their strategic planning?

Answer: Do it. To integrate forecasting into strategic planning, businesses should make it a regular part of their decision-making process. This involves using forecasts to set realistic goals, allocate resources, and anticipate future challenges. By incorporating forecasting into their strategic planning, businesses can make more informed decisions and adjust their strategies to stay on track.

Question: What common errors do businesses make when creating forecasts?

Answer: Common errors in forecasting include not creating forecasts at all, setting unrealistic growth expectations, assuming unrealistic improvements, and failing to understand past performance. To avoid these mistakes, businesses should base their forecasts on historical data, market trends, and realistic assumptions. Regularly reviewing and adjusting forecasts based on actual performance also helps maintain accuracy.

Question: How can businesses ensure their forecasts are both ambitious and realistic?

Answer: Know where you are and where you have been. Businesses can ensure their forecasts are both ambitious and realistic by grounding them in a thorough understanding of their current financial position and historical performance. This involves analysing past trends, identifying key drivers of performance, and setting achievable targets. Regularly revisiting and adjusting forecasts based on actual results helps keep them realistic while still pushing for growth.

Action Items
- Understand why a forecast is so important.
- Prepare a forecast for your business.
- Use the forecast to run your business and make better decisions.

Chapter 11: Cash and Funding

NOTES

As I stated at the beginning of this book, I have two rules for running any business:

> Rule 1: Focus on Cash
>
> Rule 2: Don't forget Rule 1

This shows the importance of cash in any business and brings it to the fore.

Remember what Michael Dell said about cash:

"We were always focused on our profit and loss statement. But cash flow was not a regularly discussed topic. It was as if we were driving along, watching only the speedometer, when in fact we were running out of gas."

Cash is the fuel your business needs.

You cannot afford to run out of cash or your business dies.

Fact.

Don't forget it.

Remember how many businesses were profitable when they failed?

Why did they fail?

They ran out of cash.

3 Daily Questions

Remember my 3 daily questions to ask first thing every morning in your business to keep cash as the focus of everything you do:

- Question1: How much cash do we have?
- Question 2: Who has our cash?
- Question 3: How do we get more cash?

I apologise for the repetition, but I cannot reiterate this enough.

So, please remember:

1. My 2 Rules for running any business.
2. My 3 daily questions.

They create a focus on cash and are a constant reminder of the importance of cash.

Many businesses approach me when cash is very tight and they have lots of stress in their life, but also lots of other opportunities that they are unable to take advantage of.

What do I do at that stage?

Understand the business, its people, and its model, and find the best way of getting more funding into it.

Is it that simple?

Yes.

The obvious question is: How do you get more cash or funding to finance growth?

Answer: from banks and investors.

How do you do that?

What do banks and investors need to know?

They need to know:

- Where you are.
- Where you have been.
- Where you are going.

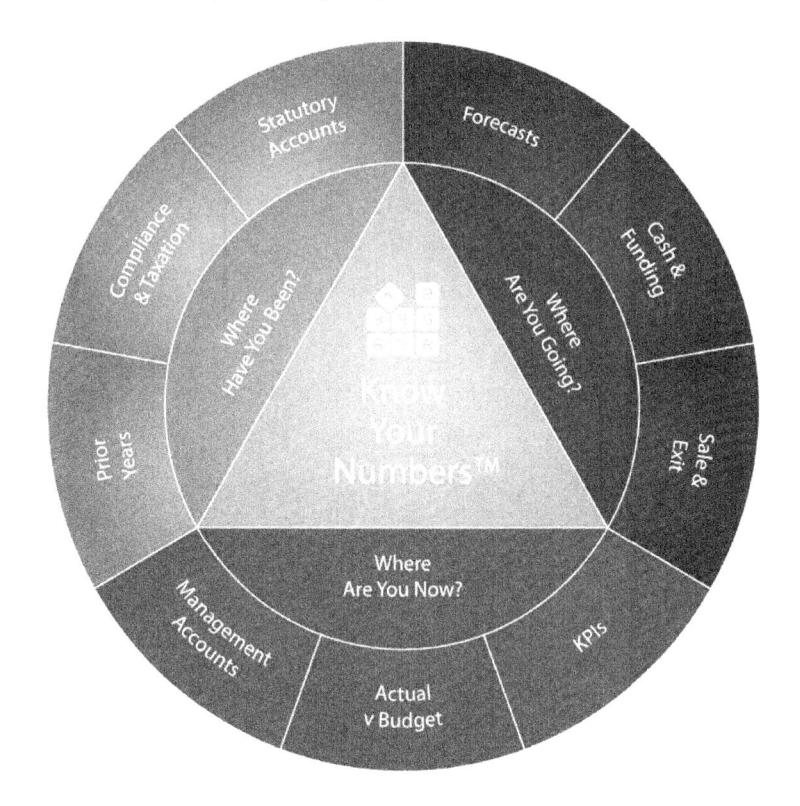

It's as simple as that.

It is exactly the same information you use in your business to improve it and to make better decisions.

That is exactly what the bank and/or investors require.

To make it even easier and show exactly what the information is:

Know Your Numbers

- Where you are – management accounts
- Where you have been – historic statutory accounts
- Where you are going - forecasts

The funders will generally want to know a bit more about the business too. What you do, who you do it for, who else does it, who is in your team, etc.

Business Plan Framework

I have created a very simple framework for a business plan that I have used for many years (see Appendix 4).

Many people think of a business plan as a long and detailed document of 30, 40, 50 or even 100 pages and that is what gets you the funding.

Nonsense.

The business plan and the financial information gets you a meeting.

Too long and full of jargon and it will be ignored.

Keep it brief, concise and to the point. Avoid jargon.

I like to use the following sections, all of which are generally one page (two maximum):

1. Executive Summary
2. Background and The Opportunity
3. Products and Services
4. Market and Competitors
5. Business Strategy
6. Key Differentiators and Risks
7. Management and Shareholders

8. Financial Information

9. Conclusion

10. Appendices

That's it.

Show that you know your business.

Show you are different.

Show you have a team to deliver.

Show that you Know Your Numbers - current, historic, and future.

You must have a forecast.
Otherwise, how do you know how much funding you require?

How can you tell the bank/investor how much cash you need without a forecast? You can't.

Remember my question about how do you run a business without a forecast? Badly.

Similarly, how do you raise more finance without a forecast? You don't.

If you have a profitable business, a good management team and this information then you will secure funding. However, you must show what you need, what you will do with it, and where it will take you.

That's what a forecast does. Trust me.

Banks and investors only make money from lending and investing it. They want to do that.

You must show them that you are a good opportunity for them.

Example: "Bill & Ben"

I've been called many things over the years, mainly by my second wife and many accountants. Let me tell you a story about "Bill & Ben."

They had been trading for a year with a turnover of £1m and had ambitions to grow to £10m in 3 years.

They engaged me to raise a working capital facility and to work with them on an ongoing basis. We secured £500,000 on very good terms. However, they decided against it due to the cost and the belief that all customers paid within 7 days.

I warned them about what could happen if customers stopped paying within 7 days, but they insisted, saying, "they won't."

I told them that if they were serious about growing to £10m then they should take the facility.

This is where they called me condescending!

Six months later, they faced a cash issue as the 7-day payment terms weren't adhered to. Within a year, they went into liquidation. In my view, you can never have too much cash or working capital facilities. Put them in place before you really need them – in order to do that, you need to look forward and understand where you are going.

What is the difference between banks and investors?

Banks
Banks are the key source of funding for your business growth. They provide loans and working capital facilities (such as overdrafts and invoice finance/factoring facilities) to many businesses.

Remember, banks only make money when lending to companies, so they are always keen to do so, but only to companies that are a good risk.

To secure bank lending, it is important to show that you and your company are a good risk.

How do you improve your chances of securing bank funding and being viewed as a good risk?

If you can show the bank:

- Where you are
- Where you have been
- Where you are going

You may be familiar with this now!

And you can convince them that you have an effective strategy and a good management team to deliver the operational plan, then they will lend to you all day long.

I like to ensure my clients do the following:

1. Show the bank that you understand your financials and more importantly, your cash flows.
2. Show the bank that you prepare good financial information timely and regularly (historic, current, and forecast).
3. Keep the bank close. Share regular information, ideally share your management accounts package and updated forecasts monthly, as well as having a regular discussion (perhaps quarterly). Tell them the good news and share the bad news – but explain the bad news and what you have done about it to turn it from bad news into good news (or at least acceptable news that does not unduly

worry the bank). Let them know you are aware of it and are dealing with it rather than hiding from it).

What types of funding do banks provide?
Banks can offer a variety of funding, including:

- Commercial mortgages: Used to purchase property related assets like production facilities, service depots and offices; usually repaid over 20+ years.

- Business loans: Similar to mortgages, but not secured on property and usually based on the assets of the company and the future cash flows; usually repaid between 3 and 7 years.

- Asset finance: Used to purchase assets used in the business, such as plant and machinery, production equipment, IT equipment, trucks and vans, tools and equipment, office equipment and cars; usually repaid over 3 to 5 years depending upon the asset life.

- Invoice Finance/Factoring: These facilities convert your debtor book into cash immediately, usually based on a percentage of the invoice value from 40% to 90%. It is a great way to finance growing profitable businesses.

- Overdraft: An agreed excess cash position that the business can operate to, secured on the general assets of the company and, usually, by a guarantee from the owners and directors.

Loans and asset finance facilities are repaid over a set number of years and attract an interest charge and agreement fee, too, which is all agreed at the outset and before signing documentation.

Invoice finance/factoring facilities are generally put in place for a period (usually 12 months and renewed annually), and attract a monthly interest charge and an administration fee. Some providers also offer the ability to insure customer debts if they don't pay and that attracts an additional fee.

Banks receive their money back and make a small margin on that lending.

It is important to match the right funding to the situation that requires the financing. As outlined above there are specific types of financing and structures for different situations, and most banks will adhere closely to this.

As a business owner, it is important that you understand these structures and your obligations with respect to security, repayment and what happens if things go wrong.

Unless you have a professional and experienced adviser in your team or a part-time/fractional Chief Financial Officer (CFO) or Finance Director (FD) I encourage you to take expert advice before making any such decisions. You may also want to speak to fellow business owners and learn from their experiences.

I am an advocate of debt funding for the right situations as it is can be more appropriate and cheaper, but as mentioned above, it does come with risks if you fail to repay on time. Too much debt in the business increases the risk profile of that business so be careful and seek specialist advice.

Investors

Investors are different and invest in the company by buying shares and becoming a part-owner too (shareholder). They are generally seeking longer term returns and returns that are significantly higher as they do not receive the investment money back. They are taking a bigger risk as they do not have security on assets and, as a result, to balance that risk, they seek a higher return.

Their investment returns come from dividends (effectively a share of profits) and when the company is sold, just like you, so investors are often more aligned with you. It is important to discuss and agree timescales and plans before securing investment as it is vital that there are shared goal and timescale expectations with respect to exit and sale are aligned.

The requirements of investors are more complex than banks, but that is not something for this book.

Again, it is vital to take professional financial and legal advice when considering external investment.

Example: Funders' Requirements

What do funders need to know to assist you and provide funding?

Quite simply, the same information you need to run your business.

The secret to getting all the funding you need is in the Know Your Numbers framework:

- Where you are;
- Where you have been; and,
- Where you are going.

Have you ever had to turn away profitable work? This will not just 10x your acumen; it can 10x your business! Take advantage of opportunities. I have various clients who were stuck at around £1 million. Opportunities were there, but they couldn't fund the growth. Now, they are making between 10 and 20 times more profit.

Remember to always make it easy for finance providers.

- Give them the information.

- Show you know your business.
- Show you know your sector.
- Show you Know Your Numbers.

Simple!

Critical Points

- Building Blocks for Success: Delve into securing funding and assembling the right team for financial growth.
- The Thrill of Funding: Discover the excitement and strategic importance of obtaining the right funding.
- The Common Dilemma: Address the typical challenges businesses face when they lack the cash or financial strategies to engage funders.

Conclusion

Understanding and managing cash flow and funding options are pivotal to maintaining financial health and supporting business growth. By mastering these areas, you can better position your business to withstand financial challenges and seize new opportunities.

Take the time to review your current cash management and funding strategies. Are there opportunities for improvement?.

Frequently Asked Questions

Question: What funding sources do you find are often overlooked by businesses?

Answer: Many businesses overlook a variety of funding sources, including government grants, angel investors, venture capital, and crowdfunding. Business owners often focus on traditional bank loans and may not be aware of these alternative funding options. Exploring a diverse range of funding sources can provide businesses with the capital they need to grow and innovate.

Question: How can businesses better prepare for discussions with potential investors or lenders?

Answer: Businesses can prepare for discussions with potential investors or lenders by thoroughly understanding their financial position and using the Know Your Numbers framework. This involves having detailed and accurate financial statements, clear cash flow forecasts, and a well-thought-out business plan. By demonstrating a solid grasp of their financials and future prospects, businesses can build credibility and increase their chances of securing funding.

Question: What advice would you give to a business that is struggling to manage its cash flow effectively?

Answer: Read the Mastering Cash Flow book, listen to the 3 daily questions, and implement them.

Expanded **Answer:** For businesses struggling with cash flow management, it's essential to educate themselves on best practices. Reading relevant books, such as my "Mastering Cash Flow: How Business Owners Can Banish Stress & Sleepless Nights, And Secure Funding For Growth!" and implementing practical strategies like the 3 daily questions (How much money/cash do we have? Who's got our money/cash? How can we improve our cash position?) can significantly improve cash flow management. Regularly monitoring cash flow and making adjustments as needed is crucial for maintaining financial stability.

Question: Are there lesser-known funding options that businesses typically overlook?

Answer: While many businesses may not be aware of various funding options, the most effective approach is to thoroughly research all available sources. This includes traditional bank loans, government grants, angel investors, venture capital, and crowdfunding. By exploring all potential funding avenues, businesses can find the best fit for their needs and growth plans.

Action Items

- Remember my 2 Rules for any business – I do not apologise for repetition.
- Remember the 3 daily questions.
- Work closely with funders, and keep them close, to ensure you have a properly financed business.

NOTES

Chapter 12: Sale and Exit

NOTES

What is Your Number?

There is another question I like to ask my clients.

"What is Your Number?"

So, I'll ask you too.

What is Your Number?

Often this is met with a confused look.

What do you mean? My number? My mobile number?

No, your Sale and Exit number?

What is that?

How much money do you want to sell your business for and when?

Ah, that makes more sense now.

However, in most cases, the business owner has never thought about it.

Wealth is not a subject that is often discussed.

Neither is retirement and the future. Both tend to go into the "too difficult" box.

The focus for most business owners is generally on the day-to-day matters and how to pay the wages next week.

Think about it a bit more.

What is Your Number?

This is the Number that means you do not have to work again and the number that allows you to look after everyone and everything you want to.

You never have to think about money again.

It doesn't have to be based on reality.

It's Your Number.

What I do when I have that Number is we discuss it.

Why is that Your Number?
How flexible are you with respect to the amount and the timing?

Then the real fun begins.

We start working backwards from that Number and creating a plan that gets us to it.

Often, it is not as difficult as you many think.

Example: Charlie
Would you like to de-risk your life financially?

What is your number?

That is the number you need to live your life without worrying about cash and looking after children, grandchildren, etc.

That's the number to focus on – not what you think the business is worth.

Charlie was told his business was worth £100M. I asked him what his number was – he said, "I own 30%, so £30M."

I laughed and said, "you'll never spend £30M. What's your real number?"

Often, it is £10K or £20K per month, that is the number.

He changed from £30M to £10M very quickly and then got to £5M.

I am not trying to discourage ambition, instead my point is not to stay in too long and don't be greedy. I am working with various clients where we are de-risking and getting some cash out. Think about what your number is. Focus on it and don't be greedy.

Company Valuation

Now, before we go further we need to think about valuing a company.

How do you value a company?

Like many accounting and finance related things, there is no right or wrong answer to this, and the value of a company is ultimately what a willing buyer and a willing seller decide on the valuation through negotiation.

However, there are a number of different areas we can look at that impact and influence valuation.

Please remember that there is no right and wrong and that valuation is all about opinions.

If you ask 3 different accountants for a valuation of your business, you will probably get at least 6 different answers!

What I want to do here is create an awareness of what is considered in a company valuation.

Various ways of valuing a company include:

Price Earnings Method

Price Earnings Method (multiple of profits) uses a multiplier that is applied against the profit figure. Now, as you will have seen there are various different profit figures – EBITDA, profit before tax, profit after tax and retained profit. In this scenario, it is important to be clear what profit is being used. Similarly, is it last year's figure, this year's, next year's forecast or the last 12 months' profit?

There can be huge variations in these figures. Be clear. Know Your (Profit) Numbers!

Adjusted Profit Figure

There is another added complication where we exclude large one-off items to create an adjusted profit figure.

Why?

The acquirer is effectively acquiring the future revenue stream of the business – what is known as the Future Maintainable Earnings ("FME") so generally the multiple will be applied to that adjusted profit figure.

So, if you've had something that does not happen every year, adjust for it. For example, moving premises, a fire or flood, and any additional costs that do not recur.

This is to your advantage and can substantially change the adjusted profit figure.

What about the multiple?

Whilst companies listed on a recognised stock exchange will have a relevant multiple, private unquoted companies do not as the shares are not traded.

This is another area of confusion.

What multiple do we use?

Good question!

It depends!

Without creating a full chapter on corporate finance and valuation techniques, there are often recognised ranges of multiples for companies. The other method is to find a comparable listed company and use its multiple discounted by 40% to 60% and use it.

As I said at the start of this section, it depends!

- **Recognised Industry Basis** – many sectors or industries have a recognised way of valuing companies. For example, a professional services business is normally valued on a multiple of turnover of anywhere between 0.5 times and 1.5 times. There are many others.

- **Comparable Valuation** - consider the value of comparable companies that have sold in recent times or whose value is already in the public domain.

- **Discounted Cash Flow** – this is generally applied to mature businesses that are heavily invested and have predictable and stable cash flow in future years. The discounted cash flow method estimates what a future stream of cash flow is worth today. The valuation is the sum of these discounted cash flows forecast for each of the next 15 or so years plus a residual value at the end of the period.

- **Comparable valuation** - this method uses the exit value of comparable companies that have sold in recent times and whose value is already in the public domain. That is often the difficult part – "in the public domain" as many private company sales are kept confidential, and the structure is not disclosed.

- **Entry Valuation** – this method values a business by estimating the cost of starting up a similar business and the costs of entering the sector.

- **Asset Based Valuation** - used for loss making businesses or businesses with sizable assets,. both tangible and intangible.

Having said all of the above on valuation, my preferred approach is a bit different.

Not everyone agrees with my approach!

You decide what you want to sell your business for.

It does not need to be a detailed valuation.

Remember, it is your Number.

It is not for you to justify it.

It is for the buyer to justify the basis of it to its board and/or shareholders.

A different approach – yes?

Of course, your Number has to be based on reality.

There is no point saying you want £10 million for a business that is making £50,000 a year.

You must be realistic.

And the best way to get to your Number?

Create competition.

Ensure there is demand for your business.

This comes back to my differentiation point. I will discuss value drivers below too and how you can increase the value of your business.

If your business is unique and has something that others don't have, then that drives up the value.

A high gross margin is indicative of that – you set the price rather than compete on price or take the market price.

What are the key drivers of business value?

I've mentioned two that I like to focus on – based on my two favourite numbers – Gross Margin and EBITDA.

What other things drive the value of a business?
Differentiation

I talk a lot about differentiation.

If your business is not differentiated, then you are what I call a "me too" business and you compete on price.

Think about it.

If a customer can get the same thing you provide from the business next door and the one next door to that, and so on, then price is likely to be the deciding factor because you are all selling the same thing.

However, if the customer can only get what you sell from you, then you no longer compete on price.

There is a demand for what you have and a scarcity factor because only you provide it.

What does that mean?

It means you set the price.

That means you make more money and have a high gross margin – assuming you have priced it correctly!

That makes your business more valuable.

It impacts positively on your profitability, cash flow, and business/shareholder value.

Competitive Advantage

As I discussed briefly above, a high gross margin is a crucial factor for investors and potential acquirers as it indicates that a company has established pricing power through marketing differentiation and possesses a competitive advantage. A strong competitive advantage is an indicator of a company's long-term sustainability, making it more appealing to potential investors.

Think about Apple compared to its competitors. Apple has a highly differentiated product which creates a strong competitive advantage and allows it to charge higher prices. It's highly differentiated product and brand is controlled through its stores and the buying experience. Many of its "competitors" provide "me too" products and compete on price thereby generating lower gross margins and possess significantly lower business value as a result.

Growth

Growth is generally important to an acquirer too. Usually, larger companies buy smaller companies, and they want to turn the smaller company into a larger company, or at least integrate it into what they provide and use their existing networks. Therefore, to show that you are in a growing market helps particularly if you can show an abundance of opportunities. A larger company should generally be able to take greater advantage of these opportunities as a result of greater resources.

Historical Financial Performance

Historical Financial Performance is a strong indicator too. If you can show that you have successfully grown, usually on the back of limited resources as you are a smaller company, then you can show the acquirer how much more you could grow with their resources, infrastructure, and support.

Future Maintainable Earnings

As mentioned above FME is important. If you can show differentiation, a pattern of successful growth and an abundance of opportunities going forward then that is attractive to an acquirer.

An acquirer is not buying your historic performance – they are buying your future performance and earnings. That is why I like to base exit values on future profitability – if you can show in your forecast where you are going and can show a high degree of delivering on forecasts historically then you can argue for higher sales values. Often exit structures will involve a payment on completion and a deferred element which is based on future performance – this "earn out" can be attractive if there is future growth, but it has to be within your control.

Management Team
I asked at the start if you have a job or a business. Do you work in the business or on the business? If you are thinking of retirement you must build a management team that can run the business on a day-to-day basis without you. Within that management team, you do not want to be too heavily reliant on one person either. By having an effective management team in place, it allows you to agree to a shorter handover period and to enjoy your exit proceeds.

Reliance on Key Customers and/or Suppliers
If you have one customer that is 80% of your business or one key supplier where you purchase most of your materials, this restricts the value of the business as it creates more risk. What if something happens to these key businesses? I encourage clients to have a good spread of both customers and suppliers and not to be overly reliant on any.

Recurring Revenue
Think of Sky, Netflix, or mobile telephone companies. They have ongoing contracts with their customers and know with a high degree of certainty what revenue will be next month, the following month and so on. If you have that in your business then that increases value. A good order book helps in this area too. Why? It reduces risk and provides more certainty of future trading.

Working Capital

As discussed above this is the funding you require in the business to meet day-to-day obligations. Think of an acquirer. They need to make two payments if they are buying your business – one to you and the other to fund the working capital. This means that if you have a high working capital requirement then the exit payment to you is likely to be lower. The way to avoid this is to have good credit control and a low element of trade debtors and a low level of stock and work in progress, with corresponding good credit limits and payment terms with suppliers.

There are other drivers of value, but for me these are the important ones to focus on.

Critical Points

Get them right and your valuation will increase.

- Identifying Your "Number": I encourage readers to reflect on their financial goals and the importance of de-risking.

- The Power of Cash Flow: I want to emphasise daily cash management and its role in preparing for a profitable exit.

- Navigating Industry Challenges: Brainstorm strategies for dealing with common hurdles in preparing a business for sale or transition.

Conclusion

Exiting a business is as significant as starting one. With proper planning and execution, selling your business can be a rewarding and profitable endeavour that sets the stage for your next chapter in life.

If you're considering selling your business or planning an exit, start preparing today. Engage with financial and legal advisors to ensure you are well-prepared when the time comes.

Frequently Asked Questions

Question: What are the key factors to consider when planning an exit strategy?

Answer: When planning an exit strategy, key factors to consider include the desired sale price, the timing of the exit, and identifying potential buyers. It's important to have realistic expectations regarding the value of the business and the timeframe for selling it. Conducting a thorough valuation, understanding market conditions, and preparing the business for sale are essential steps in planning a successful exit. Know your exit number and when you want it.

Question: What are some key legal considerations that businesses often overlook when planning an exit?

Answer: Key legal considerations that businesses often overlook include ensuring all financial records are up-to-date, understanding tax implications, and having clear contracts and agreements in place. It's crucial to work with legal and financial advisors to ensure all aspects of the sale are covered, from due diligence to finalising the sale agreement. Proper legal preparation can prevent complications and ensure a smooth transition.

Question: How can businesses best prepare their operations for a potential sale from day one?

Answer: To prepare for a potential sale from day one, businesses should maintain accurate and detailed records of all financial transactions, operations, and legal agreements. This includes keeping up-to-date financial statements, contracts, and compliance documentation. By implementing strong record-keeping practices and maintaining transparency, businesses can make themselves more attractive to potential buyers and facilitate a smoother sale process. It should be part of running your business, not just something you do for sale preparation.

Action Items
- Calculate "your number" and have a plan to achieve it.
- Be aware of the different ways of valuing a company.
- Understand the key drivers of business value and implement them in your business.

SECTION 5 – LEARN MORE

NOTES

Chapter 13: Learn, Apply & Grow

NOTES

Throughout this book I have mentioned three key principles:

- Learn
- Apply
- Grow

Execution: The Key to Success

Like many things, execution is the key to success.

You must take action.

You must apply your learnings.

Otherwise, you will have a little more knowledge, but still be in the same position as you are now.

I assume that is not the purpose of reading this book.

So, do something about it.

Think again about a few things.

Reflect on Your Past Decisions

What financial decisions have you made previously that you would change if you had the right facts and information?

Erroneous assumptions you made.

No information.

Even worse, the wrong information.

Things that cost you money.

Opportunities that you missed or didn't make you as much money from as you anticipated.

Tolerance in Your Business

Remember.

Know Your Numbers

You get what you tolerate.

What have you tolerated in your business that has not helped you?

What have you not put in place that you should have?

Use this opportunity to make changes to your business.

Implement Systems for Success

As I have said throughout this book, it is not difficult.

Hopefully, I have shown you that you must:

- Put the systems in place.
- Generate the information.
- Measure and monitor.
- Have accountability.
- Do everything every day.
- Have a specific measurable plan.
- Rely on real time information.
- Monitor variances.

The Importance of Measurement

Measurement allows you to see what improvements or corrections are required.

Variance reports – positive do more; negative make changes.

Business is complex and the future is unknown.

Nobody has all of the answers.

Nobody has a crystal ball.

But, we can help ourselves by doing all of the things I have spoken about.

Decision-Making Based on Information

Surely you want to make decisions for your business based on the best information?

- Know where you are.
- Know where you have been.
- Know where you are going.

I like to think of the process as quite simply:

- Where are you now – management accounts
- Where have you been – historical accounts
- Where are you going – forecasts

These are all simple to put in place. They are also simple to understand. Use them in your business.

Without this, your business will probably stall due to lack of funding and lack of confidence from the bank and other funders, or indeed fail.

This is the result of poor financial management and no effective strategy or plan.

It doesn't have to be that way.

You may have numerous opportunities from existing customers and new potential customers, but you will be unable to access these and deliver them without Knowing Your Numbers.

Improve the reporting culture within the company internally and externally, and align the operational and financial plans. They are your map to success.

I have shown you how to do it.

There is no point in having great up-to-date financial information if you do nothing with it.

The key point is to ensure you have the right information and you use it to make better decisions

This provides clarity, certainty, and visibility.

It will also improve profitability, cash flow, and shareholder/business value.

Business Fundamentals

Think about why you started your business in the first place.

Most businesses are based on good operational skills – very few know how to run a business and even fewer understand financials.

It has been stated that it takes 10,000 hours to become an expert in anything. You do not need to be an expert in finance, but you must Know Your Numbers.

It is your business, and it is your responsibility.

You must put the effort in and first learn and then apply.

Learn, apply and grow.

Conclusion

The learn-apply-grow cycle we focus on in our Know Your Numbers Mastery Groups is not just a business strategy but a mindset that should permeate all levels of an organisation. By embracing continuous learning and adaptability, businesses can achieve not only growth but also longevity and relevance in their industries.

Assess your organisation's approach to learning and growth. Are there opportunities to enhance how you learn from experiences and apply these lessons? Take proactive steps to integrate continuous learning into the core of your business strategy.

Frequently Asked Questions

Question: What learning resources do you frequently recommend to business owners?

Answer: To continuously improve their financial literacy and business acumen, business owners should actively engage with learning resources such as the KYN framework and relevant books. Recommended readings include works by industry experts that provide practical insights and strategies for managing business finances effectively. Staying informed and applying new knowledge is crucial for ongoing growth and success. Think of your personal development, too.

Question: How can businesses create a culture that supports continuous learning and application?

Answer: It comes from the top. Creating a culture that supports continuous learning and application starts with leadership. Business leaders should model a commitment to learning, encourage their teams to seek out new knowledge and provide opportunities for professional development. By fostering an environment that values growth and improvement, businesses can drive innovation and maintain a competitive edge.

Question: What are the best practices for implementing changes based on new learning?

Answer: Do it. The best practice for implementing changes based on new learning is to take immediate action. Once new information or strategies are identified, businesses should develop a clear plan for implementation, assign responsibilities, and set measurable goals. Regularly reviewing progress and making adjustments as needed ensures that new practices are effectively integrated into the business operations.

Question: How can businesses measure the impact of the learning and growth initiatives?

Answer: The impact of learning and growth initiatives can be measured by tracking changes in key financial performance indicators. Metrics such as revenue growth, profit margins, cash flow, and return on investment (ROI) provide tangible evidence of the effectiveness of new strategies and practices. By monitoring these indicators, businesses can assess the value of their learning initiatives and make data-driven decisions for future improvements.

Action Items

- Take action and apply your learnings in your business.
- Put the right systems in place.
- Make decisions based on information.
- If you want to take your learning further, register your interest in joining one of our Know Your Numbers Groups at knowyournumbers.biz.

Chapter 14: Know Your Numbers Framework

NOTES

The Framework

It is not complicated. The Know Your Numbers Framework is all you need to master your finances.

Think of it as a map for your journey.

Let's assume that today, we are all going to Aberdeen. However, we are all starting in different places. Therefore, our maps will be different, and knowing the starting point is vital. Otherwise, the journey we take will not be right and we will not reach our destination.

We must know our starting point. This is exactly like our forecasts and looking forward.

We can use the past to assist with the forecast assumptions. Most accountants look back, but the truly successful and most valued finance professionals look forward.

Where are we going, and what resources do we need? A question I like to pose: how do you run a business without a forecast? The answer: badly.

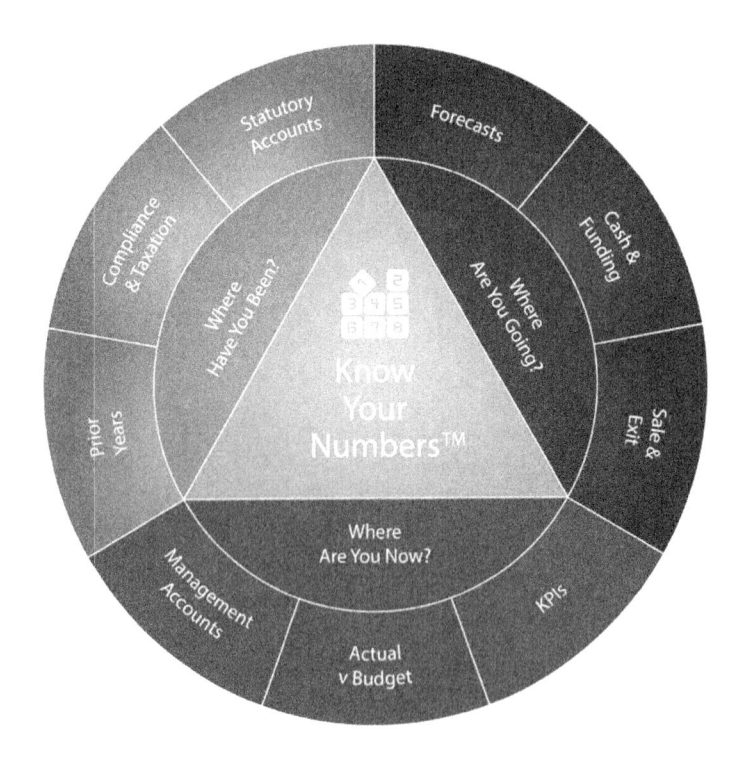

Understanding the Know Your Numbers (KYN) Framework

The Know Your Numbers (KYN) Framework helps you understand:

- Where are you now?
- Where have you been?
- Where are you going?

Knowing Your Numbers means that you will always have the confidence you need to make sound management decisions.

Join Know Your Numbers at knowyournumbers.biz.

In today's competitive business environment, understanding the core financial metrics of your enterprise isn't just helpful—it's essential. The "Know Your Numbers" approach isn't just about keeping tabs on your finances; it's about integrating this knowledge into every aspect of your business strategy. This chapter unpacks this philosophy, showing you how to apply it to enhance your business' performance and sustainability.

Core Concepts of "Know Your Numbers"

"Know Your Numbers" revolves around several key financial metrics that every business owner should master:

- Profit Margins: Understanding how much money your business actually keeps from its sales.

- Cash Flow: Monitoring the actual cash entering and leaving your business.

- Operating Expenses: Keeping a close eye on the costs involved in the day-to-day running of your business.

- Revenue Growth: Tracking the rate at which your business's income is increasing over time.

These numbers are crucial for making informed decisions and steering your business towards financial health and growth.

Integrating "Know Your Numbers" into Daily Business Practices

To effectively integrate these principles:

- Daily Monitoring: Use tools and software to track these numbers in real-time.

- Regular Reviews: Schedule weekly or monthly meetings to review these metrics and adjust strategies accordingly.

- Employee Training: Ensure that your team understands these numbers and their impact on the business.

Case Studies and Testimonials

Successful businesses across various industries have leveraged "Know Your Numbers" to their advantage. There are many on the Know Your Numbers website at: kynmastery.com/kyn-book-resources and also in Chapter 15.

Overcoming Challenges with "Know Your Numbers"

Common challenges include:

- Complexity of Financial Data: Simplify data through dashboards and visualisations.

- Resistance to Change: Foster a culture that values data-driven decision-making.

- Lack of Financial Expertise: Invest in training or consult with financial experts.

The Role of Technology in "Know Your Numbers"

Technology plays a pivotal role in this approach:

- Accounting Software: Tools like Xero and QuickBooks provide essential data at your fingertips.

- Business Intelligence Systems: Platforms like Tableau or Microsoft Power BI can help visualise complex data and reveal trends.

Enhancing Decision-Making with "Know Your Numbers"

This approach improves decision-making by:

- Providing Real-Time Insights: Make quicker, more informed decisions with up-to-date data.

- Identifying Trends: Spot opportunities and threats early by tracking changes in key metrics.

Conclusion

Adopting the "Know Your Numbers" approach transforms how you manage your business, turning raw data into actionable insights that drive success. It's not just about understanding your financials—it's about using that understanding to make smarter decisions that propel your business forward.

Take the first step today by reviewing how well you understand and monitor the key financial numbers in your business. Consider tools or services that could enhance your ability to track these metrics effectively.

Frequently Asked Questions

Question: Are there any additional 'numbers' or metrics that you think should be included in this chapter?

Answer: The metrics covered in this chapter provide a comprehensive overview of the key financial indicators that businesses should monitor. These include revenue, expenses, profit margins, cash flow, and various performance indicators. By focusing on these fundamental metrics, businesses can gain a clear understanding of their financial health and make informed decisions.

Question: What common pitfalls do you see in how businesses interpret these numbers?

Answer: Common pitfalls in interpreting financial numbers include failing to understand what the numbers mean, not knowing which key numbers to focus on, and not recognising which numbers can be influenced by their actions. To avoid these issues, businesses should invest time in financial education and work with financial advisors to gain a deeper understanding of their financial data. This knowledge empowers them to take proactive steps to improve their performance.

Question: What steps should businesses take to ensure they are correctly implementing the KYN framework?

Answer: To ensure correct implementation of the KYN framework, businesses should follow the guidance provided in this book. This includes regularly reviewing key financial metrics, conducting variance analysis, and making data-driven decisions. Additionally, businesses should seek professional advice when needed and continuously educate themselves on best practices for financial management.

Action Items

- Remember to focus on profit margins – high gross margin generates more profitability and results in a more valuable business.
- Know Your Numbers – where you are, where you have been and where you are going.
- Remember my 2 Rules.

NOTES

NOTES

Chapter 15: What People Say

Here's what members say about being part of a Know Your Numbers Mastery Group

"Everyone setting up a company at Companies House should be made do Know Your Numbers!"

John Hillis

"The Know Your Numbers course was monumental. It didn't just improve my understanding of finances - it made me a better businessman."

Ben Achampong

"I can't recommend Know Your Numbers highly enough if you actually want to know what your figures mean and how to plan and run your business better. Craig is the matrix for numbers and is in my legends category."

Ian Chapman

"Within weeks of working with Craig, I completely transformed how I manage cash flow and forecasting. The impact on my business was immediate and significant."

Jordan Howard

"Before Craig's programme, financial reports were like a different language to me. Now, I can finally understand the numbers and use them to drive my business forward."

Shaun Dunn

"Craig showed us the importance of gross margin across our range of services and customers and it's now a key number we monitor… it's been a game changer for us."

Sue Yildiz

"Know Your Numbers is an absolute must if you're intimidated by your accounts or cash-flow in any way. Craig helps to demystify the jargon and provides business owners with the tools they need."

Dr David Brennan

"Craig's approach is incredibly personable. He breaks everything down to a level that anyone can understand - whether you're a business owner or sitting across from a head of finance."

Allan Dempsie

"The Know Your Numbers programme gave me the confidence to make tough decisions. It was eye-opening to realise when it was time to walk away from a failing business - and that decision transformed my focus for the better."

Rebecca Sutherland

"Everything's more focused now. Focused on clients, on profitable business. We're now very good at deciding what work we want and what kind of work, more importantly, we don't want!"

Bobby Sutherland

"It helps you make the right decisions for the business, right from day one! You're looking at things from a totally different mindset"

Peter Rigley

"I found Know Your Numbers invaluable. The format was fun, interactive, and inclusive. Craig has a way of making numbers less overwhelming and helps apply them to real life business challenges."

Gayle Robertson

"We had never used forecasting in our business and had no idea how to properly forecast previously and now we run our business by our weekly rolling cash flow and our monthly integrated forecast, focusing on variances and changes. It's invaluable!"

Gennine Cope

"Know Your Numbers was incredibly helpful. It makes financial concepts easy to understand and apply in any business. Craig is incredibly knowledgeable and uses real-world examples to put his teaching into practice. I feel more confident in my understanding of business financials.

Highly recommend!"

Stewart Smith

Chapter 16: You've Read the Book, What Now?

NOTES

Taking Action: The Next Step
Reading this book is the easy part – now take action and implement your learnings in your business.

Don't be a business owner who avoids Your Numbers.

And remember, they are Your Numbers.

It is Your business and Your responsibility.

Don't be one of the 80% that fail due to not managing cash.

Demystifying Financial Management
I hope that I have removed the mystique and the black art perpetrated by accountants.

Knowing Your Numbers is simple.

Great business owners aren't born with business knowledge or finance knowledge.

Accountants and finance professionals typically do not teach you and explain.

Successful business owners do something different.

They study, practice, and build teams.

Leaders are learners.

You have shown that you want to learn.

The future is unknown.

However, we can reduce risk by having the right information.

Education Requires Execution
Education without execution is pointless.

I assume that at the start of this book, you did not Know Your Numbers.

How do you feel now?

I told you it was simple.

Go armed with your new knowledge and make changes.

The key to success is consistency of execution – doing the right things at the right time.

Remember, doing ordinary things consistently can create extraordinary results.

Avoiding Common Pitfalls

Don't be another technically gifted operational business owner who fails or misses out on opportunities.

The best roofer or house builder often falls down in respect of business and a failure to Know Their Numbers.

Many good businesses have failed or not optimised returns due to this failure

It's a bit like Karaoke – just because you have the words doesn't mean you can sing.

You now have much more information.

Information that I know works if applied.

Mastering Your Numbers

It has been said that it takes 10,000 to become a master in something.

You don't need to be a master in Knowing Your Numbers.

Just apply these simple tools, techniques, and ideas.

If you really want to move to the next stage, then why not join a Know Your Numbers Group?

Wishing You Success

I wish you every success in your business journey.

I am confident that by Knowing your Numbers it will be a much more enjoyable and profitable experience.

Thank you for taking the time to read Know Your Numbers – remember it is only the start. The next part is up to you to take action.

<u>Craig Alexander Rattray</u>

Action Items

- Run your business with the right numbers and make better decisions.

- Join a Know Your Numbers group.

- Remember – Knowing Your Numbers is simple!

NOTES

SECTION 6 - APPENDICES

NOTES

Appendix 1: Glossary of Terms

Accruals
Accruals are expenses where the invoice has not yet been received. An adjustment is made in the profit and loss account to bring in the expenditure in the right period as a cost and to reflect it in the balance sheet as an amount due. This is reversed when the invoice is received.

Break-Even Point
The point at which total revenues equal total costs, meaning the business is neither making nor losing money. It is not a position to aspire to, but it is useful to understand. It is usually referred to as a level of turnover, but it is a level of turnover at a particular average gross margin. Both need to be understood to establish the break-even point.

Business Plan
A document outlining a company's strategy for achieving its goals. It does not need to be a huge document. In my view, less is more. The template provided shows my preferred format with sections limited to one or two pages maximum, with all details in the appendices.

Prepayments
A prepayment is an expense that has been paid, but not yet incurred. An example is quarterly rent. If the rent due for the quarter is £3,000 and is invoiced and paid on 1st January for the period to 31 March, then at the end of January £2,000 has been prepaid. An adjustment is made to reflect this and charge the P&L £1,000 per month in each of the 3 months from January to March. This results in a prepayment of £2,000 at the end of January and £1,000 at the end of February. Without this adjustment, January would incorrectly show a cost of £3,000 and zero in February and March.

Work In Progress

Work In progress or WIP, accounts for costs incurred at the end of a period and not yet invoiced to the customer. This ensures that costs and income are matched in the same period. When the job or project has been completed, this entry can be reversed and thus ensure that costs and income are matched in the same period.

Working Capital

Working capital is the funding/cash that a business requires to meet its day-to-day trading and operational costs. It is usually financed by way of cash, overdraft or invoice finance facility.

Appendix 2: Accounting Conventions

Introduction

Accounting conventions are standardised guidelines that govern the methods and practices of financial accounting. Understanding these conventions is essential for anyone involved in business and reviewing financial statements, as they ensure that financial statements are both accurate and comparable across different periods and entities.

I like to focus on five main principles that underpin accounting practices and the preparation of financial statements. These are the accrual principle, the matching principle, the historic cost principle, the conservatism principle and the principle of substance over form.

Fundamental Accounting Principles

- **Accrual Principle:** This principle states that economic events should be recognised in the financial statements at the time they occur, not when cash is exchanged. This approach gives a more accurate picture of a company's financial position regardless of when cash is exchanged. This is the basis on which most financial statements are prepared.

- **Conservatism:** Accountants and business owners should always err on the side of caution when faced with uncertainty. This means recognising expenses and liabilities as soon as possible when there is uncertainty about the outcome, but only recognising revenues when they are assured.

- **Consistency:** Once a company adopts an accounting principle or method, it should continue to use it from one financial period to the next. This consistency allows for the comparison of financial statements over time and ensures that users of the financial statements or information are able to make meaningful conclusions from the data.

- **Going Concern:** This assumption is that the business will continue to operate for the foreseeable future unless there is evidence to the contrary. This affects decisions about asset valuation, depreciation methods, and more. The going concern principle is the assumption that a business will continue to exist in the near future, in other words, that it will not liquidate or be forced out of business.

- **Matching Principle:** Income and expenses relating to the same matter should be reported in the same accounting period. For example, if a company builds houses, the costs of building the house should be reported in the same period as the income is recognised. This can be done using prepayments, accruals, and work in progress.

Conclusion
A solid grasp of accounting conventions is crucial for anyone managing business finances. These standards not only guide the preparation of financial statements but also ensure that the information presented is reliable and consistent over time.

Call to Action
Review your business's financial practices in light of these accounting conventions.

Appendix 3: Is Your Cash Flow Limiting Your Growth?

One of the greatest constraints business owners face is cash flow. Without sufficient cash, even the most promising businesses can struggle to grow, invest, or seize opportunities. As I often say, cash is the lifeblood of your business. Yet, so many business owners are flying blind, unsure of whether their cash flow is holding them back.

This is where our new 'Is Your Cash Flow Limiting Your Growth?' Scorecard comes in.

Why Focus on Cash Flow?

Cash flow is often the silent killer of businesses. It can leave you sleepless at night, constantly firefighting rather than planning for growth. But when you truly understand your cash flow, you're in a position to make informed decisions - not guesses. You can spot issues early, identify opportunities, and create a more sustainable, stress-free business.

Over my 30 years of working with businesses, I've seen the transformative power of mastering cash flow. From helping owners pay themselves properly to enabling them to confidently invest in their growth, the impact is huge. That's why I've something with actionable insights: the 'Is Your Cash Flow Limiting Your Growth?' Scorecard.

The 'Is Your Cash Flow Limiting Your Growth?' Scorecard

This scorecard is a simple, yet powerful tool designed to help you determine if cash flow is limiting your growth. By answering a number of targeted questions, you'll uncover hidden risks, identify strengths, and gain clarity on what's holding your business back.

Here's how it works:

- Answer the straightforward questions about your current cash flow practices and outcomes.
- Get your personalised score and insights, showing you exactly where you need to focus.
- Take action based on your results, with clear steps to improve your cash flow and unlock your growth potential.

The scorecard removes the guesswork and makes it clear where you stand. It's an essential step in moving from reacting to proactively managing your business finances.

Don't Let Cash Flow Hold You Back

Your cash flow can either propel your business forward or hold it back. The good news? You're in control. The 'Is Your Cash Flow Limiting Your Growth?' Scorecard helps you take that control and provides a clear roadmap to move forward.

So, are you ready to find out if cash flow is holding your growth back? Take the Scorecard now and let's start solving your challenges together: iscashflowlimitingyourgrowth.com.

Remember my two rules:

Rule 1: Focus on cash.

Rule 2: Don't forget rule 1.

By mastering your cash flow, you'll unlock growth, reduce stress, and start making the kind of decisions that lead to a more profitable, enjoyable business. Let's make that happen.

Appendix 4: "MY BUSINESS PLAN TEMPLATE"

Contents

1. Executive Summary
2. Background and The Opportunity
3. Products and Services
4. Market and Competitors
5. Business Strategy
6. Key Differentiators and Risks
7. Management and Shareholders
8. Financial Information
9. Conclusion
10. Appendices

    i Financial Projections and Assumptions for the period to XXXX

    ii [Other Information that should not form part of the main narrative – details, examples, brochures, CVs, technical explanations, detailed market information etc.]

NOTES

Appendix 5: Gross Margin Versus Mark-Up

This causes confusion for business owners.

It is vital to understand the difference and ensure that you are not talking at cross purposes with a customer or supplier.

What is the difference between Gross Margin and Markup? They both focus on the same amount of money – the difference between your buying and selling prices, and they both express that amount as a percentage. However, Gross Margin is expressed as a percentage of income while Mark-Up is based on the cost. Hence, for a profitable business, Mark-Up will always be higher than Gross Margin.

The Gross Margin formula is:

Gross Margin = Gross Profit / Revenue as a percentage.

The Markup formula is:

The Markup Formula = Gross Profit / Cost of Sales of Direct Costs.

Your markup is always bigger than your margin (for a profitable business), even though they refer to exactly the same amount of money.

Markup tells you how much you increase the cost of the things you sell or materials you recharge

Margin tells you what percentage of income is gross profit.

Gross Margin Definition
Gross Margin is sales minus the cost of goods sold. For example, if a product sells for £100 and costs £70 to manufacture, its margin is £30. Or, stated as a percentage, the Gross Margin is 30%.

Mark-Up Definition

Mark-Up is the amount by which the cost of a product is increased in order to derive the selling price. To use the preceding example, a markup of £30 from the £70 cost yields the £100 price. Or, stated as a percentage, the markup percentage is 42.9% (calculated as the markup amount divided by the product cost).

Comparing Margin and Mark-Up

It is easy to see where a person could get into trouble deriving prices if there is confusion about the meaning of margins and markups. Essentially, if you want to derive a certain margin, you have to markup a product cost by a percentage greater than the amount of the margin, since the basis for the markup calculation is cost, rather than revenue; since the cost figure should be lower than the revenue figure, the markup percentage must be higher than the margin percentage.

Example

Sales   £100

Cost of Sales £80

Gross Profit   £20

Gross Margin = Gross Profit/Sales = 20/100 = 20%

Mark Up = Gross Profit/Cost of Sales = 20/80 = 25%

Markup and Margin Table

Margin	Markup	Multiplier	Margin	Markup	Multiplier	Margin	Markup	Multiplier
1%	1.01%	1.010	26%	35.13%	1.351	51%	104.09%	2.041
2%	2.04%	1.020	27%	36.99%	1.370	52%	108.32%	2.083
3%	3.09%	1.031	28%	38.89%	1.389	53%	112.78%	2.128
4%	4.17%	1.042	29%	40.83%	1.408	54%	117.40%	2.174
5%	5.27%	1.053	30%	42.87%	1.429	55%	122.21%	2.222
6%	6.38%	1.064	31%	44.92%	1.449	56%	127.29%	2.273
7%	7.53%	1.075	32%	47.07%	1.471	57%	132.58%	2.326
8%	8.70%	1.087	33%	49.27%	1.493	58%	138.10%	2.381
9%	9.89%	1.099	34%	51.51%	1.515	59%	143.90%	2.439
10%	11.11%	1.111	35%	53.83%	1.538	60%	150.00%	2.500
11%	12.36%	1.124	36%	56.27%	1.563	61%	156.40%	2.564
12%	13.63%	1.136	37%	58.72%	1.587	62%	163.18%	2.632
13%	14.94%	1.149	38%	61.29%	1.613	63%	170.29%	2.703
14%	16.28%	1.163	39%	63.92%	1.639	64%	177.79%	2.778
15%	17.64%	1.176	40%	66.68%	1.667	65%	185.71%	2.857
16%	19.04%	1.190	41%	69.50%	1.695	66%	194.11%	2.941
17%	20.49%	1.205	42%	72.41%	1.724	67%	203.01%	3.030
18%	21.96%	1.220	43%	75.42%	1.754	68%	144.50%	2.125
19%	23.47%	1.235	44%	78.67%	1.788	69%	222.59%	3.226
20%	25.00%	1.250	45%	81.81%	1.818	70%	233.31%	3.333
21%	25.75%	1.226	46%	85.19%	1.852	71%	244.81%	3.448
22%	28.20%	1.282	47%	88.69%	1.887	72%	257.11%	3.571
23%	29.83%	1.299	48%	92.30%	1.923	73%	270.39%	3.704
24%	31.58%	1.316	49%	96.09%	1.961	74%	284.60%	3.846
25%	33.33%	1.333	50%	100.00%	2.000	75%	300.00%	4.000

Margin	Markup	Multiplier
76%	316.69%	4.167
77%	334.80%	4.348
78%	354.51%	4.545
79%	376.20%	4.762
80%	400.00%	5.000
81%	426.30%	5.263
82%	455.59%	5.556
83%	488.21%	5.882
84%	525.00%	6.250
85%	583.70%	6.867
86%	614.30%	7.143
87%	669.20%	7.692
88%	733.30%	8.333
89%	809.10%	9.091
90%	900.00%	10.000
91%	1011.10%	11.111
92%	1150.00%	12.500
93%	1328.60%	14.286
94%	1566.70%	16.667
95%	1900.00%	20.000
96%	2400.00%	25.000
97%	3233.30%	33.333
98%	4900.00%	50.000
99%	9900.00%	100.000
100%	20000.00%	200.000

Know Your Numbers   199

NOTES

SECTION 7 – MEET THE AUTHOR

NOTES

Craig Alexander Rattray

With a career spanning three decades, **Craig Alexander Rattray** isn't your average Finance Director or Chief Financial Officer. He's a strategic thinker, a master with financial strategies that actually work, and an expert at raising finance and driving rapid business growth.

His unrivalled blend of skills – developed in private equity/venture capital investment management and at the coal face of supporting small businesses – along with his background as a Scottish Chartered Accountant means that Craig Alexander brings a wealth of insight and skill to the growth-focused companies he works with.

Craig Alexander thrives on supporting companies experiencing change and challenge, including early-stage development, growth, new market entry, acquisitions, and scale-ups as well as positioning for exit.

His focus is unwavering: to drive profitability, improve cash flow, and massively increase shareholder value.

He launched Know Your Numbers: a programme designed to help business owners dramatically improve their financial and business acumen, and improve the profits and cash flow in their business (knowyournumbers.biz)

He is also the author of *Mastering Cash Flow* (masteringcashflowbook.com), and *Lessons From the Rocking Chair*, as well as the host of the popular *Know Your Numbers* podcast.

Follow Craig Alexander on LinkedIn

linkedin.com/in/craig-alexander-rattray/

SECTION 8 – OTHER BOOKS BY CRAIG ALEXANDER RATTRAY

The journey of running a successful business can be pretty tough. These books aim to guide you throughout that journey.

Mastering Cash Flow: How Business Owners Can Banish Stress & Sleepless Nights, And Secure Funding For Growth!

Take a few seconds and imagine never worrying about cash flow again.

What would that do for your business and for you personally?

Available at Amazon.com or get a free PDF copy at:

masteringcashflowbook.com

Lessons from the Rocking Chair: How Business Owners Can Master Their Entrepreneurial Journey Using Timeless Wisdom and Insight

An insightful exploration into the heart of entrepreneurship, guided by the seasoned wisdom of Growth Strategist Craig Alexander Rattray.

This book dives headfirst into wide-ranging topics,

Craig Alexanders narrative, full of personal anecdotes and practical advice, underscores the significance of building meaningful relationships, embracing continuous learning, and maintaining financial acumen.

Entrepreneurs at any stage will find in these pages a blueprint for not only surviving the entrepreneurial landscape but thriving within it, all while fostering personal growth and financial stability.

Through a blend of reflective questions and actionable insights, readers are encouraged to embark on a journey of self-discovery and strategic business transformation.

Available at Amazon.com

NOTES

WELCOME TO A NEW WAY OF RUNNING YOUR BUSINESS

Knowing Your Numbers and mastering them is the key to success and enhancing the value of your business.

You will make better decisions based on facts and information rather than guessing – better decisions will result in increased profitability, cash flow, and business/shareholder value. As a result, you will have less stress and owning your own business will be much more enjoyable.

You cannot have financial freedom without financial discipline. I know it works and so do my clients and Know Your Numbers members:

> *"Thank you so much for having me in your group. I have learnt more in two hours than I have in 35 years as a business owner."*

Another business owner of 15 years said *that:*

> *"Know Your Numbers has changed my business and me as a business owner forever."*

You can join them and transform you and your business too. Running a business is not easy – if it was, everyone would be doing it.

If you Know Your Numbers and follow the learnings from this book *and apply them* in your business, your business will change forever, and so will you.

More profit, more cash, a more valuable business and less stress. Who doesn't want that? Read on and I'll show you how.

knowyournumbers.biz

Printed in Great Britain
by Amazon